ON THE
GUARD

THE YMCA LIFEGUARD MANUAL

D1716211

YMCA OF THE USA

Library of Congress Cataloging-in-Publication Data

On the guard.

Information in this ed. replaces information found in
National lifeguard manual, 1974, and Aquatic safety and
lifesaving program. 1974.
   "Published for YMCA of the USA by Human Kinetics
Publishers, Inc."—Copr. p.
   Bibliography: p.
   1. Lifeguards.   2. Life-saving.   3. Aquatic sports—
Safety measures.   I. Forsten, D.I., 1955-
II. Murphy, Marjorie M.   III. YMCA of the USA.
IV. National lifeguard manual.   V. Aquatic safety and
lifesaving program.
GV838.72.063 1986   797'.028'9   86-1731
ISBN 0-87322-059-5

Produced by: Program Development, YMCA of the USA
              Jerry Glashagel, Director
Developed by: Majorie M. Murphy, National Aquatic Program Director,
              YMCA of the USA Program Services

Editors: D.I. Forsten and Marjorie M. Murphy
Developmental Editor: Linda Anne Bump
Copy Editor: Olga Murphy
Production Director: Ernest Noa
Design: Julie Szamocki
Typesetter: Sandra Meier
Illustrations: Dick Flood
Text Layout: Janet Davenport
Cover Design: Jack W. Davis
Cover Photo: Chris Perry
Photographic Coordinator: Gary Guertin
Printed by: Phillips Brothers

Special thanks to the Aquatics Safety Task Force who worked together to make this project a reality: Rick
Celotto, D.I. Forsten, Millard Freeman, Gary Guertin, Kathy Rhoads, and Stormy Webster.

CONTENTS

FOREWORD

The contents of this book, *On The Guard*, which reflects the current revision of the YMCA Lifeguard Training Program, is the culmination of many years of commitment by YMCA aquatics professionals. The YMCA believes that the prevention of an accident and the saving of a life is worth the countless hours of training and dedication essential to become a competent lifeguard. President Roosevelt once said, "It is not the critic who counts; the credit belongs to the person who is actually in the arena . . . ," and it is with this in mind that we take the opportunity to express our appreciation to YMCA aquatics professionals all over the country who, through their time and dedication, have contributed to the development of today's YMCA aquatic safety programs.

A special heartfelt thanks is given to Charles Silvia and Thomas Cureton. Their work, started over 40 years ago, has shaped the trends of aquatic safety worldwide. We share new thoughts and problems because of the changing world we live in, but the basis for the evolution of new aquatic techniques was founded on research work of Charles Silvia, Thomas Cureton, and their colleagues at Springfield College. It is a great honor to acknowledge their work and to have the opportunity to build on it.

Additional thanks are expressed to John I.T. Moloney, Charles Arnold, and James R. Cornforth and their respective aquatics committees whose work on the past revisions of the YMCA lifesaving/lifeguarding materials has also contributed greatly to the development of this edition.

We hope that our contribution to aquatics safety will help those who follow in our footsteps as much as we have been helped by those we followed. President Roosevelt continued his statement by saying, "Who strives valiantly, who errs and often comes up short again and again . . . who at best, knows in the end the triumph of high achievement, and at worst at least fails while daring greatly." We are proud to have had the opportunity of serving the YMCA aquatics community.

Aquatics Safety Task Force
Rick Celotto, Millard Freeman, Gary Guertin, Kathy Rhoads, Stormy Webster, chairperson, and D.I. Forsten, editor

Marjorie M. Murphy
National Aquatic Program Director
Program Services Divison
of the YMCA of the USA

chapter 1

THE IMPORTANCE OF AQUATIC SAFETY

YMCA aquatic professionals have led the crusade for improved aquatic safety for over 100 years. Today, through a variety of instructional aquatic programs, the YMCA continues to enhance the quality of millions of lives. YMCA programs strive to develop individuals on three levels—in body, mind, and spirit. This goal is the essence of the YMCA philosophy and is an element of its programs, making the YMCA unique among community-service organizations nationwide.

In the past 20 years, public interest and enthusiasm for water activities has exploded. These activities take thrill-seeking enthusiasts *on the water* for recreational boating, rafting, canoeing, kayaking, and sailing; *under the water* for scuba and skin diving; *in the water* for competitive swimming and synchronized swimming; and even *above the water* for para sailing. Riding the wave of the fitness explosion of the 70s and 80s, communities now view swimming activities as a vital part of a health-promoting, life-enhancing daily routine. This trend toward aquatic activity has generated a new awareness of water fun and safety for all age groups.

Over the years, the number of drowning deaths has been on the decrease. However, it is still the third leading cause of accidental death in the United States, claiming an average of 7,500 lives each year. Of these victims, approximately 40% drown while swimming in indoor, outdoor, or backyard pools or at camps, lakes, rivers, beaches, and swimming holes. About half of these occur while the swimmer is alone, in or on an unguarded pool or beach. Between 1,000 and 1,500 drownings occur in or around a guarded area. The other 60% of the victims are nonswimmers who never intended to go in the water. These drownings include accidents in bathtubs, driving off bridges, and fishing, boating, canoeing, sailing, skating, and scuba incidents as well as accidentally falling into backyard pools.

Of the 4,500 nonswimming victims, approximately 1,300 drown in boating accidents. U.S. Coast Guard statistics reveal that 92% of people who boat do not wear personal flotation devices (PFDs). The Coast Guard estimates that of this group of victims, 80% could have survived had they worn PFDs. In addition, statistics have shown a marked increase in alcohol- and drug-related drownings from 20 years ago. The Coast Guard estimates show that for boating accidents, 50% of the drowning victims had blood alcohol levels above the legally intoxicated level.

The Y's Role

The YMCA and other community agencies have taken on the challenge of providing swimming instruction and aquatic safety training for all ages. The national YMCA has developed swimming programs from Preschool through

Scuba. Local Ys sponsor "Learn to Swim" campaigns to encourage everyone to become aquatic safe. There is little the professional lifeguard can do to prevent the accidents that occur in unguarded areas; however, educating the general public of the dangers of aquatic accidents and their prevention through YMCAs, schools, and other agencies can help reduce these numbers.

The YMCA has been teaching people to swim for 100 years and has been making significant contributions to aquatic safety for over half those years. In fact, the YMCAs have launched an intensified campaign to target programs to meet the aquatic demands of every aspect of the community from Aquatic Safety through the YMCA Lifeguard Training programs. Course information is included in Appendix A and B. The historical development of aquatic safety is summarized as follows:

Royal Humane Society	1774
Massachusetts Humane Society	1786
U.S. Coast Guard Lifesaving Service	1871
YMCA entrance into teaching	1885-90
Lifesaving Program, Springfield College	1911
National YMCA Lifesaving Service	1912
First American lifesaving text	1913
Red Cross lifesaving training	1914
YMCA Lifesaving & Swimming Manual	1929
Cureton-Silvia test text	1939
YMCA Lifesaving & Water Safety Instructor's Text	1940
Silvia's YMCA Lifesaving & Water Safety Today	1965
New YMCA Aquatic Safety & Lifesaving Text	1974
YMCA Aquatic Safety & Lifesaving Program	1979
On the Guard: YMCA Lifeguard Manual	1986

With the growing trend in aquatics, it has become necessary to scrutinize the roles of *lifesavers* and *lifeguards*. Though they share the same prefix, lifesaving and lifeguarding describe two different areas of aquatic responsibility. A *lifesaver* is an amateur who, because of uncontrollable circumstances, stumbles into an emergency situation and reacts to protect his or her own safety and/or possibly that of someone else. A *lifeguard*, on the other hand, is a professional who by definition has accepted the responsibility of protecting the safety of those in an assigned area. Lifeguards have a moral and professional obligation to prevent potential accident situations by enforcing the rules/regulations of their aquatic setting. At the same time, they are highly qualified to react to emergencies. The information found in Table 1.1 illustrates some distinctions between the lifeguard and lifesaver that should make their roles more clear.

Table 1.1   Comparison of Lifesaver and Lifeguard Roles

Lifesaver	Lifeguard
• Reacts to an accident, acting after the fact	• Acts to first prevent the accident; does react to emergency
• Reacts from a moral principle only	• Acts under a moral and legal duty
• May be covered by the Good Samaritan Laws	• Can be found liable and negligent in a court
• Does not need certification	• Must be certified by an accredited agency as required by law in some states; or qualified and trained by an individual in that facility or setting
• Has general training and is an amateur	• Is a professional with specific training for specific locations, with specific procedures for emergencies
• Usually has no special equipment available	• Has specific rescue equipment for that aquatic setting

Though the roles of lifesavers and lifeguards differ in aquatic safety, they do share a common goal—to prevent accidents and to save lives in and around the water. To be a good lifeguard, you must first know how to be a good lifesaver.

The purpose of *On the Guard* is to help the aquatics professional as well as the aquatic enthusiast understand the elements of water safety. It will provide lifeguards and aquatic leaders basic information upon which to base their experience. This manual, however, is only a start, for it is only one of a lifeguard's many tools. Nothing can replace experience and practice to help make you water safe. Each aquatic environment has unique circumstances and potential hazards, and a lifeguard's responsibility is to be familiar with and qualified for his or her own environment. Public safety will demand it. *On the Guard* gives information that lifesavers *should* know, but that lifeguards must know and understand.

Everyone who comes in contact with water should be concerned about water safety. You no longer have to go to the seashores to catch a wave or to a mountain stream to ride the rapids. In addition to the traditional pools, surf, lakes, and rivers, water parks are springing up all over the country, adding a new dimension to the aquatic environment. Now, children and adults alike can "catch a wave" in a wave pool or "ride the rapids" down a waterslide every day of the week! Surfers can take to a lake with a sail on their board and sail off into the sunset with or without the waves. Never before has this variety of aquatic opportunity been so easily accessible to so many.

Unquestionably, this aquatic explosion has opened up a whole new world of fun and excitement. To keep it that way, let's all learn how to be aquatic safe.

Review Questions

1. What makes YMCA aquatic safety programs unique from those of similar organizations?
2. Of the 7,500 drownings that occur on the average each year, approximately how many occur around guarded areas?
3. What is the primary responsibility of a lifeguard?
4. Compare the roles of a lifeguard and a lifesaver.
5. List five differences between a lifesaver and a lifeguard.

chapter 2

PERSONAL SAFETY

Aquatic knowledge and understanding are the primary tools for preventing an accident situation that could lead to a drowning. Your knowledge of the basic survival skills, safe swimming rules, PFD's, simple nonswimming rescues, and fitness and conditioning are the keys to understanding how to be aquatic safe. A strong background in lifesaving skills is the first major step in developing lifeguarding skills. To be a good lifeguard, you must first develop the basic skills. As a professional lifeguard, your actions will often speak louder than your words. Swimmers will look to you for guidance. Your understanding of personal aquatic safety will help develop the professional standard of care necessary for lifeguarding today.

Basic Survival Skills

All individuals who work and play on and around the water owe it to themselves and to their families to be able to perform minimal survival skills and to insist that their families be trained as well. A person cannot be considered water safe until he or she is comfortable in deep water.

Buoyancy

To become more comfortable in water, it might be helpful if you understand why a body does or doesn't float. Physiologically, it depends on the ratio between the specific gravities of your body and the water. Specific gravity is the ratio of equal amounts of mass (in this case, body) and fresh water. If the specific gravity of the mass is less than 1, it will float; if it is greater than 1, it will sink. Fresh water has a specific gravity of 1. The human body is made up of different specific gravities added together: muscle tissue, 1.085; bone, 1.9; adipose tissue, .7 to .98; and air, which has a specific gravity of almost 0.

Positive buoyancy refers to people who, when they add all of the specific gravities of their body, have a specific gravity of less than 1; those people will be able to float. Negative buoyancy refers to those whose specific gravity is greater than 1; they cannot float. Many who have trouble floating in fresh water would find no trouble at all floating in the sea water because it has a greater specific gravity than fresh water.

Because the legs are comprised mostly of muscle and bone, it is not likely that they will float, unless there is sufficient adipose tissue under the skin. When floating, therefore, it is a good idea for the swimmer to concentrate on the thoracic region, or more specifically, the lungs. Breath control is the single most important element swimmers can regulate in order to control their buoyancy.

The test shown in Table 2.1 was designed to determined a swimmer's ability to float. The swimmer should adopt a tight tuck position in the water, take a breath, and submerge the head. The swimmer must stay in this position as long as possible.

Table 2.1   Buoyancy Test

Swimmer's Position in the Water	Buoyancy Rating
The swimmer will bob right to the surface.	Double positive (+2)
The swimmer will slowly return to the surface.	Positively buoyant (+1)
The swimmer will remain wherever the swimmer settles after taking a breath and tucking the head.	Neutral (0)
The swimmer will slowly sink to the bottom.	Negatively buoyant (−1)
The swimmer will sink right to the bottom.	Double negative (−2)

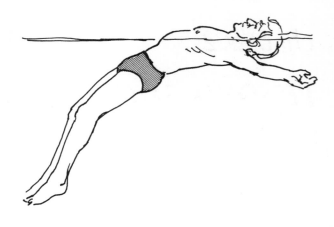

2.1   Back float

Back Float

The back float is a relatively simple skill that can be used for survival purposes. To float on your back, roll from the front prone position to a back supine position, keep your head back, and relax in the water. You will probably find your legs sinking. As they sink, arch your back slightly and take a deep breath. Your face is all you really need to keep out of the water. A slow, relaxed sculling (stroking) motion with your hands will help keep you afloat and will also provide slight propulsion. This will cause your body to balance around your lungs (see Figure 2.1).

Survival Float

Since Fred Lanoue developed his program for teaching drownproofing, many variations on the actual technique have been experimented with and found to be successful. Drownproofing enables you to float in a relaxed position almost endlessly, even without the use of your legs or arms. After taking a breath, let your body submerge. Your arms and legs should hang down in a relaxed manner, and your back should be near the surface. Hold your breath only as long as you want to. Don't wait until you need a breath. When you decide to breathe, bring your arms close to the surface, separate your legs as you do when starting a scissors kick, and start

exhaling. Press down on the water with your hands, complete the scissors kick, and hyperextend your neck. Only your face should come out of the water. Take a quick breath and return to the original starting position. The technique is illustrated in Figure 2.2.

Treading Water

Treading water, shown in Figure 2.3, is an important survival skill that should be learned by everyone. The arm motions consist of a wide, circular sculling motion with palms turned down. The hands apply constant pressure downward as they move back and forth.

Several types of kick are used for treading water. For a *single scissors kick*, one leg (always the same one) goes forward and the other leg goes backwards. As the legs are brought together, they provide a downward thrust. A *double scissors* is the same as a single scissors kick with one exception: The leg that goes forward the first time goes backward the second time. The *breaststroke kick* as described on page 10 is one of the more popular kicks. The *egg-beater* provides the most consistent support of all the kicks, although it may be the most difficult for some. An egg-beater kick is a breaststroke kick in which the legs kick in an alternating manner instead of simultaneously.

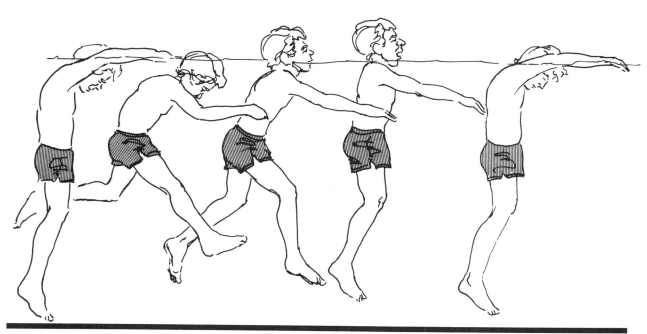

2.2 Survival float

2.3 Treading water

Experiment with all the kicks to find one with which you are most comfortable.

Inflating Clothing

The inflation of clothing is another alternative that can be used for survival if you are not wearing a PFD. The clothing must be made out of a

tightly woven material such as cotton or denim; otherwise, they will not hold air.

If an emergency occurs and you find yourself in cold water, kick to the surface, take a breath, relax into a treading position, and take off your shoes (if they hinder your kicking movement). To avoid, or at least delay the onset of hypo-

2.4   Inflating a shirt or coat

thermia, keep the rest of your clothing on. Button all buttons on your shirt except the third one from the top. Take a deep breath, lower your head (under the water), and exhale through your shirt opening. The air will rise into the opening and then will continue rising around the body to form an air pocket in your shirt. Make sure the shirt is kept tight around your neck and tucked in around your waist so that the air will stay trapped.

If you are wearing several layers of clothing or a heavy coat, lift the front of your coat away from your body, keeping it underwater. Cup your hand and forcefully plunge it into the water near the opening of your garment to push air bubbles into your clothing (see Figure 2.4). The bubbles will rise to the shoulder area, providing extra buoyancy.

Disrobing

If you are ever in a situation where you are fully clothed in the water, and there is a possibility of being able to swim to safety, you may want to take off most of your clothes, depending on the water temperature. Disrobing in the water is simple if you remember to keep calm and not to hurry the process. Assume the drownproofing position and begin by taking off your shoes. Take as many breaths as necessary. If you find yourself tiring, pause and rest for a few moments. Continue removing your clothing when you are ready. After you have taken off your clothes, you may choose to use them for extra flotation.

You can use your shirt or pants for extra flotation by using the methods illustrated in Figures 2.5 and 2.6. If you happen to be wearing both

2.5   Inflating pants-method 1

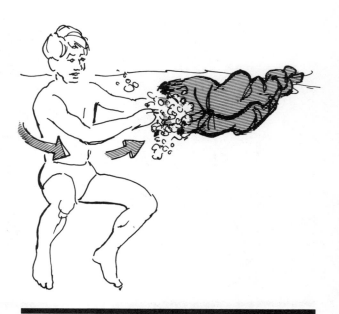

2.6   Inflating pants-method 2

shirt and pants, then it is recommended that you leave your shirt on, and inflate your pants. You may choose to inflate the shirt while still wearing it, as in the cold water situation. This aids in your flotation while removing your pants. The shirt should be kept on to help maintain body temperature. It also helps prevent the severe sunburn, which is prevalent in this type of survival situation. Lastly, if the shirt is brightly colored it can be seen more easily.

If you find yourself with only a long sleeve shirt and a bathing suit, then you can use the shirt for flotation. After removing your shirt, tie the sleeves together just above the cuffs or tie a knot in each sleeve just above the cuff. Then find the shoulder opening of the shirt, take a breath, submerge, and exhale into the sleeve. The air should make the sleeve rise to the surface. Repeat the procedure with the other sleeve. Slip your head and arms between the inflated sleeves. You can also use the methods described below to inflate a shirt.

Several methods can be used to inflate the pants. One method is to tie the legs in a square knot as close to the bottom as possible and fasten the closures; then submerge and exhale directly into the opening. Another method is similar to the method used to add flotation to your clothes in cold water: Holding the waistband in one hand, splash air bubbles into the opening with the other hand. This method is the least tiring but requires some practice. A third method is to hold the waistband behind your head and kick to raise yourself high out of the water; then fling the pants over your head and force the opening down under the surface. The air will remain trapped in the pants for at least partial inflation.

As the sun dries the cloth the air will leak out so from time to time it will be necessary to force more air under the surface and into the shirt sleeves or pant legs. Also splash water on the material to keep the garments air tight. Regardless of which method you choose, practice your first attempt at disrobing with a buddy who can help if assistance is necessary.

Personal Flotation Devices

By Federal law, a personal flotation device (PFD) is required for each person on board any small craft or boat of open construction. The U.S. Coast Guard is the public agency that establishes minimum standards for PFDs. No life jacket or vest should be purchased unless it bears the "U.S. Coast Guard Approved" tag, which is sewn on by the manufacturer (see Figure 2.7). Other flotation devices on the market, designed to serve as teaching aids, are good for that purpose and

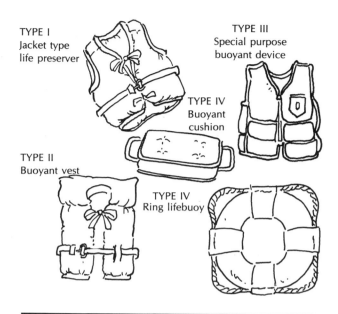

TYPE I
Jacket type
life preserver

TYPE III
Special purpose
buoyant device

TYPE IV
Buoyant
cushion

TYPE II
Buoyant vest

TYPE IV
Ring lifebuoy

2.7 Personal flotation devices (PFDs)

may be used as aids in assisting a swimmer, but only those having the Coast Guard authorization should be relied upon as personal lifesaving devices.

The four types of PFDs are Type I, good on any vessel; Type II, good on all recreational boats; Type III, good on all recreational boats; and Type IV, good on recreational boats under 16 ft and canoes and kayaks of any length.

Buoyant cushions are invaluable when used as free-floating rescue devices and provide extra comfort for boaters, but they should not be depended upon as PFDs.

Heat Escape Lessening Posture (HELP)

Critical heat loss areas are the head, the sides of the chest where there is little muscle or fat, and the groin area where major vessels are close to the surface. The HELP position will help protect these major areas by reducing the loss of heat and by slowing the onset of hypothermia in cold water. The HELP position is accomplished in the following way: While wearing a PFD, (a) float in a tuck position; (b) squeeze your legs together, crossing the ankles; (c) press your arms against your sides and hold the PFD across your chest; and (d) keep your head above the water (see Figure 2.8). This position has been found to be effective in increasing survival time by almost 50%.

2.8   HELP position

Survival Strokes

A variety of strokes that enable a person to swim to safety without becoming extremely tired are suitable for survival situations. Different situations require different strokes. In calm water, the elementary backstroke, inverted breaststroke, sidestroke, and breaststroke are recommended. In rough, choppy water, the breaststroke should be used.

Elementary Backstroke

In calm water, relax in a back-glide position. As the legs recover and initiate the kick by bending at the knees, pull your heels toward your seat, and turn your toes out. Begin arm recovery slightly before the legs recover by pulling up the sides of the body with elbows out and palms toward the body. Stretch the arms outward slightly above shoulder height, and finish the leg recovery. Pull the arms down and kick the legs slightly around and back together, pushing yourself forward in the water. This stroke will allow you to move to safety without expending much energy. The elementary backstroke is pictured in Figure 2.9.

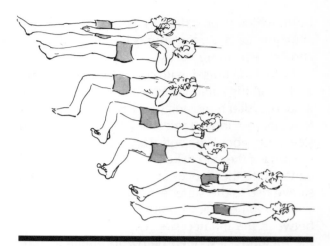

2.9   Elementary backstroke

Breaststroke

In calm or rough water, start out in a front-glide position, arms stretched in front, legs straight back. Keep your head underwater to your hairline and look forward. Keep your elbows high as you press your arms backward and slightly outward. As your hands press back, tilt your head up and take a breath. At the end of the pull as your arms recover, bend the elbow, bring the hands in front of the chin, and stretch them back to the front. Keep the palms flat, and move each palm in a motion that looks like an outline of half of a heart. To kick, pull the heels back toward your seat, turning your toes out on the recovery. Kick the legs together forcefully in a slightly rounded motion. The coordination of the stroke is, from a glide, pull (arms), breath (as legs recover), kick (as arms recover, and glide (see Figure 2.10).

Sidestroke

Start out in a glide position, sideward, with bottom arm stretched above your head in the water and the other by your side. Lean your head to the side with your ear in the water. As your legs recover together, pull your heels toward your seat. Stretch your top leg forward and your bottom leg backward; then pull both legs together to complete the kick. Pull your bottom arm down toward your body (elbow bent) and then stretch your arm back to the front. At the same time that you pull with the bottom arm, the top arm recovers (bend the elbow). Then reach with the

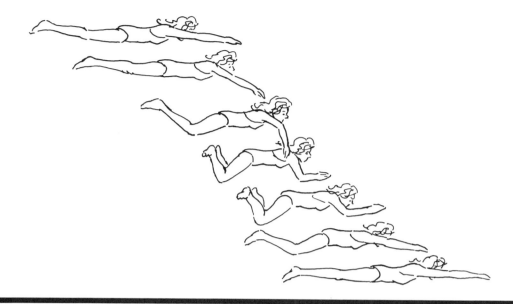

2.10   Breaststroke

hand toward the opposite shoulder and push downward. The arms work in opposition, that is, while one is stroking, the other is recovering. The kick follows the top arm: As the arm recovers, the legs recover; as the arm strokes, the legs kick (see Figure 2.11).

Nonswimming Assists

Nonswimming assists enable you to make a rescue without placing yourself in danger; consequently, they are the most highly recommended rescue techniques. Nonswimming assists

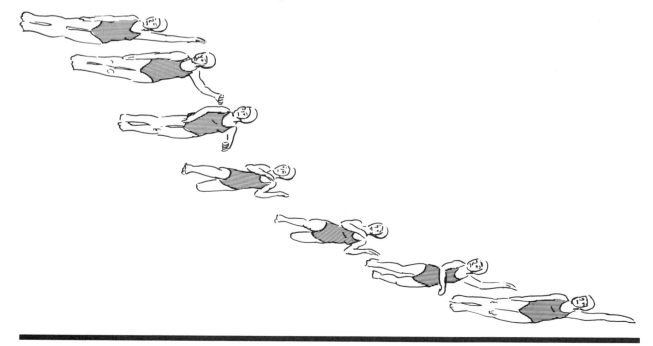

2.11   Sidestroke

can be divided into three groups: reaching and extension, throwing, and wading. When making a nonswimming rescue, maintain visual contact with the victim and find a piece of rescue equipment appropriate for the situation (like an oar, a board, or a broom handle). Use any object around the swimming facility that will allow for quick and efficient rescue; it need not be elaborate.

When making the rescue, *always guard your own safety*. Establish a firm footing or hand hold and keep body weight low and away from the victim. Remember, if you get pulled into the water, you may become a victim yourself. Establish communication with the victim by talking to him or her. Encourage the victim to help with the rescue. It will not only make it easier and safer for you, but will also reduce the victim's trauma. Once the victim is at the side of the pool or dock, help him or her out of the pool. Once out of the water, make sure the victim is uninjured before you let him or her go. If the victim's breathing has stopped, begin resuscitation immediately.

2.12   Reaching assist

Reaching and Extension Assists

Reaching assists, although limited to rescues only a few feet from the side of the pool or dock, play an important role in lifesaving. To use a reaching assist out of the water, lay on the pool deck to maintain a stable position. Spread your legs apart to increase stability. Extend *only* your arm over the water to the victim. If the victim is panicky, it may be extremely difficult to grasp the wrist because it is probably moving around frantically; instead, grasp the upper arm. Proper technique is depicted in Figure 2.12.

A second type of reaching rescue can be made by slipping into the water, establishing a firm grip on the ladder or the side of the pool, and then extending your other arm or leg to the victim, as shown in Figure 2.13. In this type of rescue, however, where you reach with your arm, make sure you grab the victim before he or she grabs you; otherwise, the victim may catch you by surprise and pull you away from the wall.

Towels, clothing, branches, pieces of wood, and lightweight chairs along with the conventional aluminum poles and shepherd's crook can

2.13   Reaching assist from in the water

be used for a quick extension rescue. When using any of these, extend the object after you have established a good foothold. Keep your body weight low and away from the victim. Be prepared for the victim to give a sharp tug as he or she grabs the object. An extremely panicky victim may not grasp the extended object. If this happens, keep the object within easy reach or slide it under the victim's armpit and press it against his or her side. Do not jab the object into the victim's chest, for this could result in injury.

After the victim grabs the object, pull it in slowly, hand over hand, so that you don't pull it out of the victim's hands. Talk constantly after you pull the victim to the side, helping him or her out of the water.

Throwing Assists

If the distance to the struggling victim is beyond the range of an extension assist and if the necessary equipment is readily available, a throwing assist may be the best option. The key to a successful throwing assist is accuracy; and the key to accuracy is practicing ahead of time. A heaving line (a line with a weighted knot on the end), a heaving jug (a plastic gallon jug with a small amount of water to give it some weight and with a line tied to the handle), or a ring buoy with a line are all acceptable throwing devices.

2.14 Throwing assist with a buoy

For example, to throw a ring buoy, hold the neatly coiled rope in an open hand. Secure the buoyant knot or attachment at the the end of the line under your foot or around your wrist. Hold the ring buoy in one hand and the rope in the other. As you throw the ring buoy underhand, let the rope feed freely from the other hand. Throw the ring buoy over the victim's head (or in a river, upstream, allowing the river to carry it downstream to the victim), and then pull it to the victim (see Figure 2.14). If, for some reason, the ring buoy moves away from the victim, plant your feet and pull in the rope, letting it drop on the ground in front of you; then throw the buoy again. Do not recoil the line, for it wastes precious time. Practice this several times during class until you become proficient. Be careful to avoid rocks, branches, or anything that could tangle the line. A trained lifeguard will probably opt to swim the buoy out to the victim to save time. However, this should only be attempted by those who have been trained to react to this situation. An untrained person who emotionally reacts to the situation is risking the possibility of becoming a second victim.

Wading Assists

In a basic wading assist, enter the water and proceed toward the victim until you reach chest-deep water. Then extend a piece of equipment or some clothing to the victim. Be careful to keep your weight shifted back away from the victim, so that when he or she grabs the object, you won't be pulled toward him or her, as illustrated in Figure 2.15. Once the victim has grabbed the buoy or whatever, slowly walk toward the shore.

2.15 Wading assist using a buoy

Keep talking to the victim and continue helping them until they are safely out of the water. This assist can be used in combination with other non-swimming assists and is more dangerous for non-swimmers because they must enter the water.

Nonswimming rescues are the most practical of all rescues. They enable both the skilled lifeguard and the novice swimmer to make an efficient rescue, minimizing their own potential danger. When a swimmer needs help, react calmly, and quickly find the nearest and most practical object that can be used for a rescue. Be prepared to give the necessary first aid once the victim is safely on the shore.

Additional Concerns

Other water-related concerns regarding health and personal safety include the fitness benefits derived from swimming and the potential hazards that the swimmer may face.

Fitness and Conditioning

Swimming has long been lauded as the most popular activity in this country. According to a recent Nielsen Sports Participation Study, 47.5% of the population enjoy swimming. Swimming is a total exercise: inexpensive, enjoyable, and less painful than land exercise. It is one of the few forms of exercise that so easily adapts to all fitness levels, from the recreational to the highly competitive. Swimming strengthens your heart, blood vessels, lungs, and muscles while increasing flexibility without the painful effect gravity sometimes has on joints. In addition to an over-all increased quality of your physical health and well-being, swimming can play an important role in weight control and in increasing emotional energies to enhance daily activities.

Cramps

When a swimmer experiences a cramp the first thing to remember is not to panic. Relax as much as possible and begin to survival float if necessary. If it is at all possible, leave the water. Cramps can be relieved more comfortably on land.

To relieve the pain of a cramp you need only stretch the cramping muscle. The stretching activity should be slow and steady, without any bouncing movements. Hold the stretch for 30 to 60 seconds for the best results. If the cramp is severe, the pain may initially get worse for a few seconds as you begin to stretch the muscle. You must continue to stretch the muscle for the prescribed amount of time. If stretched only until the pain goes away, the cramp will usually return immediately upon using the muscle.

Exhaustion

Most people who get tired will leave the pool and rest. Children, however, often get involved with their play and continue longer than they should. Before they reach this point, their parents should get them out of the water. The problem of exhaustion is more common in lakes and oceans, primarily because there are no supports to hold and often no bottom on which to stand. The beginning of the swimming season, particularly, finds some swimmers in situations they cannot handle. When they attempt to swim with the same skill they exhibited at the end of the previous season, they often experience exhaustion.

Panic

Panic can be defined as an emotional state in which a person has been overcome by a sudden overpowering terror and has completely lost the ability to reason. Panic usually occurs when a person is faced with a seemingly life-threatening emergency. For example, if a person gets a cramp while swimming and does not know what a cramp is or how to alleviate it, more than likely that person will panic and possibly drown. Knowledge is the best preventor of a panicked state. Knowing what a cramp is, that person can work to relieve it, whereas the uninformed victim might lose all reason and drown. In most swimming emergencies, panic precedes actual drowning.

Eating Before Swimming

Everyone has heard the old maxim, Don't go swimming for an hour after you eat or you'll get a stomach cramp and drown. The advice may be common sense; however, the result is less than accurate. How soon you go into the water after eating should depend upon several factors: (a) the amount of food consumed, (b) the kind of food ingested, (c) your general physical condition, (d) your degree of fatigue, (e) the water temperature, and (f) the vigor of your swimming activities. Recent studies have suggested that accidents that have occurred when people have gone swimming immediately after a large meal have not been from cramping, but from vomiting their meal and aspirating vomitus into their lungs.

After eating a large meal, most people do not feel like going swimming or participating in any vigorous activity for an hour or more. This is nature's way of keeping the body quiet so that the digestive system can start the process necessary for the absorption of the food. Normally, when you begin swimming, your blood flow is shunted away from your stomach to the muscles that need energy to maintain the swimming activity. This slows the absorption and the digestive process. For young children it is usually wise to establish a minimum amount of resting time following a meal before they are allowed to swim. Older individuals tend to regulate themselves; if they feel uncomfortable, they get out of the water or slow down their activity. All swimmers should recognize the uncomfortable feeling in the abdomen as nature's warning and govern themselves accordingly.

Review Questions

1. Name three survival skills that would help you stay afloat if you found yourself in a situation where you would be in the water for a long time.
2. Why would you want to keep most of your clothes on if you unintentionally found yourself in cold water?
3. Why are nonswimming assists important?
4. Is the old adage, Don't swim for at least an hour after you eat to avoid getting a stomach cramp and drowning, true? Why or why not?

chapter 3

GENERAL AQUATIC INFORMATION

As a lifeguard on duty, you are expected to know all, see all, and protect all with respect to your aquatic area. Of course, no one can be all. By having a basic understanding of environments and science, you will broaden your basic understanding of aquatic situations; as a result, it will be easier for you to analyze and to recognize potential dangers before they become accidents.

Every aquatic environment will have its own set of potential hazards. No matter what kind of training you have completed, you will have to take time to become familiar with the particular place you work. Knowing about these special hazards is the key to being able to protect the safety of the swimmers in that area.

Weather Conditions

Many factors come into play when you try to protect the safety of those in your area—some you can control and others you cannot. The weather is an uncontrollable factor that even meterologists have a hard time analyzing and predicting, much less trying to control. However, being able to observe certain principles will help you recognize hazardous weather before it hits you.

The weather forecast might state that a front will be moving through your area. Barometric changes and sudden shifts in the wind direction and velocity are signs that the weather will probably be changing. As the warm air meets cooler air, moisture (in the form of a rain shower or thunderstorm) usually results. Although you can't control the weather, you can take the necessary precautions to prepare for the weather changes and to protect the safety of the swimmers in your area.

Storm Conditions

Cloud formations will also alert you to potentially bad weather. Cumulonimbus clouds, shown in Figure 3.1, are dark and vertical and signify a storm. Stratocumulus clouds (see Figure 3.2) are continuous, connected globes that usually occur before and after a storm. Altocumulus clouds, like those pictured in Figure 3.3, are high and white and could signify a storm if they become large and dark. You might see a gray line on the horizon; this indicates that a squall line, the severe weather, is on the way.

Thunder clouds and lightning are serious weather conditions. Although there is little documented evidence of the effect of lightning on swimmers, the facts are clear: Your body in or touching water near a lightning strike could act as a natural conductor of electrical current from the lightning, possibly resulting in death. It's difficult to determine what constitutes a safe distance from a lightning strike. Don't take any chances when you see lightning. Follow the procedures of your facility and clear the area before the storm hits. You can estimate the approximate distance of the storm by counting the

3.1 Cumulonimbus clouds

3.2 Stratocumulus clouds

3.3 Altocumulus clouds

seconds between seeing the lightning and hearing the thunder. Because light travels approximately 186,000 mi/s and sound travels 1,100 ft/s, divide the seconds by 5 to get an estimate of your distance from the storm in miles. For example, if you see lightning 10 seconds before you hear the thunder, the storm is two miles away.

Guidelines for when to clear swimmers from the area will depend on the type of facility and on the management. If there are no procedures, encourage the staff and management to establish a standard operation for bad weather, possibly patterned after other facilities similar to the one in which you work. Once procedures are established, practice them. The safety of those in your area depend on it. In bad weather, attempt to do the following things:

- Clear and secure the area, making sure everyone is out of the water.
- Move to shelter, preferably in a building, rather than under an open structure or tree.
- Stay away from metal objects that might conduct electrical current.
- Avoid using the telephone.
- Get down from the lifeguard stands; lightning is attracted to the highest objects.
- Avoid using the showers.

High winds often cause changes in water conditions that could present a potential danger for swimmers in the water who are unaware of the change in weather. Swimming pools are not likely to be as affected by the wind as are open-water areas such as lakes, rivers, and oceans. The wind can create or enhance the size of the waves, influence currents, and reduce water visibilities. In any open-water area, wind is an element to consider.

Fair Weather Conditions

Good weather also poses some interesting uncontrollable hazards for which you should be prepared. Hot summer days usually bring people in droves to outdoor facilities. Sunburn, heat stroke, and heat exhaustion are hazards with which you will be faced. These conditions will also affect you and your ability to supervise the safety in your area. Be prepared for good weather! On hot days, wear a hat, cover your shoulders with a wet towel, wear sunglasses, use sunscreen, and keep fluids available.

Water Environments

Water temperature in open-water environments usually is layered with the warmer water on top. These levels of water temperature are called *thermoclines*. Normally the warmer water stays at the surface, but a shift in the surface temperature can cause the warmer water to cool and drop down to the lower levels. This could take a swimmer who is not used to colder water by surprise, and hypothermia could set in. Under these conditions, fatigue may set in more quickly.

In certain areas the actual condition of the water should be closely monitored, especially if industry is located nearby. In the absence of water circulation, certain conditions could make the water excessively murky. Excessive changes such as discoloration, temperature changes, dead fish, or putrid smell should be reported to local health officials. These conditions could pose a health hazard in your area. However, for every aquatic area, there are natural hazards that are unique to the area, and one chapter can not possibly cover all the information. Use this information as a general guideline and evaluate your own area.

Ocean Environments

In an ocean environment, a combination of wind and bottom conditions contribute directly to the size of the surf at any particular beach. The stronger the wind and the sharper the incline of the bottom, the larger and stronger the waves. The surf is also affected by tides. Tidal changes are water conditions that are predictable and constant. Tides are created from a gravitational pull of the sun and moon on our earth's bodies of water (see Figure 3.4).

Become familiar with the following general terms associated with surf conditions:

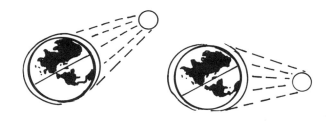

3.4   Gravitational pull and the tides

- **Set**—a series of breaking waves.
- **Lull**—a calm between sets.
- **Rolling**—gently sloping transverse waves found in deep water.
- **Capping**—wind forcing the rest of the wave over into the trough.
- **Breaking**—water pushed over the crest, particularly if near shore where the bottom slows the speeding water; also occurs when rolling waves pass over a shallow area of the bottom (such as a reef) in shallow water.
- **Peak**—the highest point of the wave at which the wave breaks right to left or left to right.
- **Foam**—(whitewater) the weight of water falling into the trough as a wave breaks, causing air to be trapped in the water; water/air mixture will support neither swimmer nor water.
- **Fetch**—the distance of open water over which any wind blows and develops waves; the greater the length of fetch, the greater the possibility of large waves.
- **On-shore wind**—wind that blows toward the shore.
- **Off-shore wind**—wind that blows toward the water; particularly dangerous for those using flotation devices, who without knowing it, could be carried from shallow water due to the wind direction.
- **Parallel**—a current of water running parallel to shore caused by waves breaking on the shore at an angle.
- **Runback**—a return flow of water swept onto the shore as waves strike; sometimes called an undertow which is somewhat misleading because the water runs back.

- **Rip/runout**—a current of water moving out to sea that is created where there are bars or reefs just off shore. The runout is the return flow of water trapped between a bar and the shore. The current picks up speed as it moves through the rip channel and back out to the ocean. A runout dissipates after passing through the break in the bar or reef.
- **Surf zone**—shallow area where the waves break.

Rip currents.   Rip currents are the most common surf condition for which a beach lifeguard must watch because most surf rescues involve swimmers caught in a rip. The channel or trough may be as much as 8-ft deep. A rip current usually looks different from the surrounding surf and is easy to spot from an elevated position. Key characteristics include the following:

- The rip may be dark and appear to be deep water.
- The water may be rough and choppy because of waves and the direction of the prevailing current opposing it.
- The rip may appear muddy or brown as a result of dirt and sand stirred up from the bottom.

- Rips have stronger force after a wave set has hit the shore.
- Persons swimming in or near this current are drawn to sea.
- A rip may have one source of water or as many as three feeder currents.

Many beach areas have permanent rips. These areas should be a key point in your watch. A fixed rip is caused by a stationary object projecting into the water (i.e., rocks, piers, drains) and may be present for a period or change from season to season. A flash rip may result from unusual wind or water conditions changing quickly. Flow from rips continually changes the bottom conditions and therefore causes hazards to those unfamiliar with the danger.

Because the current is pulling seaward, it is impossible to swim against the current without undue physical tiring. Therefore, a swimmer should move parallel to the shore until the seaward pull decreases to the point that swimming toward the beach is possible. The direction of a rip current is diagramed in Figure 3.5. For a rescue, use the rip or runout to your advantage to get out to the victim quickly. Waves very seldom break in through a rip, making it easier for you to maintain eye contact with the victim as you approach.

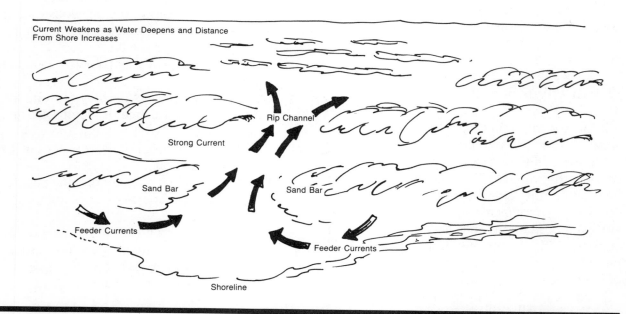

Current Weakens as Water Deepens and Distance From Shore Increases

Rip Channel

Strong Current

Sand Bar   Sand Bar

Feeder Currents

Feeder Currents

Shoreline

3.5 Rip current

Marine life.   Marine life and coral on the bottom pose potential dangers. Some aquatic animals such as jelly fish and the man-of-war have long tentacles that inflict a painful sting if you come in contact with them. Some shells and coral can inject a poison venom or inflict a sharp cut if stepped on. Reactions to these situations range anywhere from a mild sting to shock, nausea, and respiratory difficulty. If the reaction is severe, seek medical attention.

River and Stream Conditions

In rivers and streams, as in ocean environments, currents can be particularly dangerous because they have a tendency to change. This is a natural occurrence because river beds and ocean bottoms are also in a continual state of change. As the currents shift, an unsuspecting swimmer can be caught by surprise and carried away from shore before realizing what has happened. Watch out for changes in the currents and be prepared to react. If caught in a current, swim diagonally across it, never directly against it, unless the current is weak and you are swimming a short distance. Because current strength is deceptive, don't take any unnecessary chances.

Lake, Pond, and Quarry Conditions

In fresh water, underwater weeds or other plants pose a potential danger, not necessarily in themselves, but rather in the consequence or reaction of a surprised swimmer. If they panic while in contact with weeds, swimmers may become entangled as a result of frantic and erratic movements intended to free them. The danger lies not necessarily in the entanglement, but in their fright or panic. If you encounter this situation or try to rescue someone who has become entangled, use slow, subtle shaking motions to get free of entanglement. A victim who has panicked in this situation will need assistance. Encourage the victim to be calm. Bring him or her a flotation device if possible, which will provide more security and will help keep the victim's head above water while he or she is being freed. When swimming out of an area full of underwater weeds, use a modified crawl or breaststroke with minimal kicking to avoid entangling arms and legs.

Open-water areas, for the most part, are readily accessible to people in all parts of the country. Usually inland waterways are unsupervised and should be checked before swimming. Answering the following questions is important in deciding whether the area is safe for swimming.

- Are the currents too strong?
- Is there too much pollution?
- What is the marine life like?
- Is there debris around or on the bottom that provides a hazard?
- Do boats use this area?

When swimming in an open water area, check the area carefully for potential dangers. Make sure rescue and first-aid equipment, a telephone, and a rescue squad or hospital are readily accessible. Other safety equipment includes a first-aid kit and an inner tube marked "emergency equipment." In addition, *never swim alone*. A swimmer's buddy should be trained in assist techniques and capable of providing assistance to meet any emergency.

Pool Conditions

No other country in the world offers the number and variety of aquatic facilities that are now available to the public in the United States. Swimming pools provide a desirable environment for most aquatic activities. Many motel, hotel, apartment and backyard pools do not have trained lifeguards on duty. After you've been trained as a professional lifeguard, it's very difficult not to recognize potential dangers even when you are at a swimming area for your own enjoyment. *Never swim alone* in an unguarded area, regardless of your skill level in the water. If something were to happen, there would be no one around to help. Remember: *No one is immune to accidents.*

When you arrive at a pool, check for potential hazards. Is the deck slippery? How deep is the water? How deep is the water under the diving board? How is the bottom shaped? Ask these questions when you enter *any* new swimming facility—pool, lake, river, quarry, or pond.

Water parks are relatively new, developed over the past 5 years, tripling in number in the past 3 years. Over 13,000,000 people reportedly visited water parks in 1984. Realizing that these new water parks are opening up a new dimension of aquatic recreation, (adding wave pools, body flumes, and tube rides to a traditional pool), water-park owners have taken an aggressive approach to making these parks safe and enjoyable for all. To work at water parks, lifeguards must go through supplemental training specific to this new environment.

Wave pools, while offering a new "twist" to ocean surfing, do have some unique potential hazards that differ from ocean waves. These new waves are made by mechanically varying air and wind pressure and can simulate a small ocean wave. The wave machines are usually set for a series, followed by a rest. During the rest stage, the pool could become over crowded, making those in the shallow area accidental targets for body surfers when the wave series resumes. These waves can easily knock an unsuspecting person off his or her feet, posing a problem especially for younger children who might easily panic. However, with special training for these hazards, lifeguards can learn to spot these potential accidents and be ready for them.

Aquatic Science

The importance of knowing the what and why of lifeguarding plays a significant role in developing the professionally trained lifeguard. If you understand the basic principles of aquatic physiology and how it relates to different populations, then it will be easier for you to identify potential accidents, as well as to evaluate the victim's condition during that emergency. This basic understanding plus your ability to apply it to a situation is the cornerstone of analyzing an emergency. Without basic aquatic knowledge, you leave a large margin for error in your decision making

that places you and the victim in additional danger. As a professional, you are legally bound to ensure the safety of those in your keep: You must *know* and *understand* aquatics. The information provided in this section will help you begin to understand the physiology that affects aquatic safety.

Buoyancy

Buoyancy is the ability to float in water. Three principles provide information necessary to understand how and why the body is able to float: Archimedes' principle explains the physical law of buoyancy; vital capacity and center of buoyancy effect how you float.

Archimedes' principle.   Archimedes' principle states that a body (defined here as anything having mass or volume) will float proportionally to the amount of fresh water it displaces: That is, how much fresh water will a person weighing 115 lb displace? If fresh water weighs 62.4 pounds per cubic foot (lb/cu ft), then that person displaces approximately 2 cu ft of water, with 9.8 lb floating above the surface (115 divided by 62.4 equals 2, with 9.8 lb remaining; see Figure 3.6).

Because the human body is made up of muscle, bone, and fat, the density of your body can be described in terms of specific gravity. The specific gravity of fresh water is 1.0, while salt water has a rating of 1.025. The specific gravities of the major components of the human body are listed in Table 3.1. The closer the sum of the

3.6 Archimedes' principle

Table 3.1 Specific Gravities of Body Components

Component	Specific Gravity
Water	1.0
Bone	1.9
Muscle	1.085
Adipose (fat)	.70-.98

proportional specific gravities of the components of your body is to 1.0, the more buoyant you are. Notice that bone and muscle alone would sink in water because their specific gravity is higher than 1.0; they are heavier than water. Adipose tissue would float because it is lighter than water. Because people are made up of different combinations of muscle, bone, and adipose, they all float differently. The combination of these three components makes up various human body types, known as somatotypes. There are three basic somatotypes. Individuals possess characteristics from more than one of the types.

The *ectomorphic somatotype* is characterized by an individual who is very thin, has a small skeletal frame, low adipose, and low muscle content; this individual will generally be a neutral floater. The *endomorphic somatotype* is characterized by an individual who has a high percentage of adipose, or fat. This individual will generally be positively buoyant (float high in the water). The *mesomorphic somatotype* is characterized by an individual who has a high percentage of muscle; this individual will generally be negatively buoyant and will either float below the surface or not at all. How the somatotypes are combined (i.e., meso-ecto, endo-meso, meso-endo, ecto-meso) will determine an individual's ability to float.

Vital capacity. Vital capacity is the amount of air that the lungs can hold. For most, vital capacity plays an important part in floating. Air is much lighter than water. By taking a big breath, you expand the volume of the air in your lungs, causing you to displace more water, which will, in turn, enhance your positive buoyancy.

Center of gravity/center of buoyancy. The center of gravity (COG) is the center of weight of the human body. It is generally a couple of inches below the navel. The center of buoyancy (COB) is located at the chest level where the lungs are located. You can change your COB by adjusting your COG: Slowly raise your legs and adjust your arms in the water. If your arms move too quickly, they will create momentum that will cause your feet to sink. In some cases it may help to raise your fingers out of the water, adding more weight toward the head. The other action is to bend your legs to bring your feet under your buttocks. These actions move more actual weight (muscle and bone) above the COG. This, in effect, changes the COG and moves it towards the COB and helps keep the legs floating.

The Physiology of Drowning

Drowning is asphyxiation due to blockage of the trachea, usually by water, causing respiratory arrest. A drowning may occur for any of a number of reasons. While the initial reason will vary, most cases lead to panic and then progress through the four stages of drowning. *Panic* is the uncontrolled and totally incapacitating fear that strikes when someone thinks he or she has lost control. Severe panic destroys all sense of logic and rationality. Self-preservation becomes the top priority, even at the expense of friends and loved ones.

Before examining the specific stages of drowning, a brief description of the structures involved might be helpful. In the normal structure of the throat, the glottis is the top edge of the beginning of the trachea that connects to the lower part of the throat. The glottis is covered by the epiglottis, a flap of skin that acts as a plug to prevent foreign material from entering the trachea. The trachea, the windpipe, carries air from the throat into the lungs. The esophagus, the foodpipe, carries food and liquids from the throat to the stomach.

The "reflex closure of the glottis" is the uncontrolled action of the controlled process of swallowing. Normally as water enters the mouth, the tongue blocks the back of the throat. The glottis then closes, blocking the airway, the tongue drops, and the water passes the trachea (windpipe) into the esophagus (foodpipe) and to the stomach.

During the drowning process, the victim experiences first clinical and then biological death. *Clinical death* is defined as the point at which both breathing and pulse have stopped and the body is in respiratory and cardiac arrest. It is generally considered to last about 4 minutes from the time the heart stops beating. Due to the lack of oxygen, the pupils of the eyes will become dilated (widened), and the skin turns cyanotic (blue). This blueing is especially noticeable in the lips and fingernail beds. However, if the victim is revived with CPR within the first 4 minutes, there is a good chance that no brain damage will have occurred.

Biological death is the point at which irreversible brain damage begins, and the most sensitive parts of the brain begin to die. Brain cells cannot regenerate like skin and bone, so once dead, they can never be revived. Within 4 to 6 minutes brain cells will begin to die. Longer periods of oxygen deprivation result in a greater loss of brain cells.

For these reasons, it is critical for you to reach the victim and begin CPR as soon as possible. Cardiopulmonary resuscitation (CPR) maintains minimal circulation and respiration in order to sustain life until definitive therapy can begin.

The Stages of Drowning

The drowning process has been divided into four stages. Although the names of the stages may differ from text to text, the concept of each stage remains basically the same.

Stage 1: Initial apnea. *Apnea* means "no breathing." In drowning, the glottis closes by a reflex action, but unlike eating or drinking where the air supply is resumed immediately upon passage of the food or drink past the glottis, the water stays in the mouth and throat, cutting off all air to the lungs. However, no water enters the lungs. During this step, the victim's panic increases.

The time span of the first stage varies significantly from seconds up to minutes. Physiologically, the following occurs:

1. The blood pressure rises and the adrenalin flow increases due to panic and the self-preservation factor.
2. The victim begins to struggle in attempt to keep the head above water.
3. The victim swallows water into the stomach, filling some of the available air space in the body, thus diminishing buoyancy.
4. The victim gradually sinks. Each attempt to raise the head above water is less successful because of fatigue and the extra water in the stomach.
5. The brain begins to degenerate because it does not get enough oxygen to function properly (hypoxia).
6. Acidosis begins because the lack of oxygen causes an excess of waste chemicals in the blood, making the blood more acidic.

Stage 2: Dyspnea. Dyspnea refers to difficulty in breathing and occurs when the glottis begins to partially relax. Air and water begin to enter the trachea. Because the victim has swallowed water into the stomach and is growing weaker from struggling, the head will be lower in the water and more water will be swallowed. This time water flows into the lungs. If rescued during this stage, the victim would suffer from a form of pneumonia called aspiration pneumonia because of aspiration of water in the lungs.

On the surface of every alveoli (air sac) is a chemical known as *surfactant*. This substance reduces the surface tension on the alveoli's membrane, allowing for the easy exchange of oxygen (O_2) and carbon dioxide (CO_2). In drowning, the water ingested into the lungs washes away the surfactant, creating another complication to resuscitation. Because there are over 700 million alveoli in the lungs, many survive the washaway to help exchange gases as long as they are exposed to the air. The mixture of water and surfactant causes a pink froth at the mouth of some victims.

During dyspnea the victim experiences the following:

1. Aspiration of water into the lungs takes place due to the failure of the swallow reflex. While no one can intentionally swallow water into the lungs, by this stage the protective mechanism of the body has failed.
2. Because of the influx of water into the stomach and lungs, vomiting may occur in some cases.
3. Frothing at the mouth also occurs because of the mixture of surfactant and water in the lungs.
4. Brain hypoxia continues. Very little if any rationality exists at this point.
5. Acidosis continues to cause a severe imbalance in the chemicals of the blood.

Stage 3: Terminal apnea. As soon as the victim becomes unconscious and stops breathing, he or she has entered the third stage: Terminal apnea is respiratory arrest, and breathing ceases.
During this stage the following occurs:

1. Brain hypoxia continues.
2. Acidosis continues.
3. In some cases, tonic convulsions may occur in which the entire body becomes rigid, causing the victim to jerk around involuntarily; these convulsions are caused by brain hypoxia.
4. In some cases, the sphincter muscles may relax, in which case the victim will urinate and/or defecate.

Stage 4: Cardiac arrest. Cardiac arrest occurs when the heart ceases to function and pump blood. Depending on the circumstances, the third and fourth drowning stages might begin simultaneously, meaning that the heart and lungs stop together. The heart can continue to beat up to 5 min after the lungs have stopped. For this reason, artificial respiration alone can revive victims who have been under water for a short time. Once the pulse has stopped, CPR must be used to revive the victim. Clinical death begins when the heart stops.

Types of Drowning

Not all drownings happen in a stereotypic way. Various environmental conditions and situations cause different results.

Wet and dry drowning. Wet drownings comprise 80% to 95% of all drownings. This means that the glottis opened at the second stage (dyspnea) and allowed water to enter the lungs, making the lungs wet; thus, it is called *wet drowning*. The remaining drownings are dry drownings. This means that the glottis stayed shut from the first stage (initial apnea) and had no second stage.

Silent drowning. This type of drowning does not include any surface struggling because the victim is rendered unconscious, incapacitated, or dead by his or her condition. In these cases the lifeguard has no warning. This is one of the reasons the lifeguard must keep totally alert.
The following are some of the silent drowning situations.

- Heart attack
- Striking the head
- Cardiac arrest
- Shallow-water blackout (see discussion of hyperventilation)
- Stroke
- Hyperventilation blackout
- Epilepsy
- Inebriation
- Drug overdose

Laryngeal drowning. In some cases the victim may become sick and vomit while swimming. The swimmer may aspirate the vomitus into the lungs, thus choking and drowning. This has been found to be a possible cause in some of the drowning accidents related to those victims who have eaten big meals immediately prior to swimming, supporting the idea of waiting an appropriate amount of time before swimming. It is also possible for the victim to vomit in the second stage, which is a form of laryngeal drowning.

Salt- and freshwater drowning. As far as the lifeguard is concerned, there is no significant difference in the method of rescuing a victim of saltwater or freshwater drowning. When a victim drowns in salt water, the water in the blood plasma diffuses through the membranes of the alveoli because the salt (sodium) content of the water is much higher than that of the water in the blood. Because sodium attracts water, the water in the plasma is drawn out of the blood and into the lungs.

In extreme cases, the victim's blood volume can drop almost 40%. Because of the sodium imbalance, this 40% drop is critical. As water is drawn from the plasma, the blood gets thicker and the red blood cells shrink. Consequently, the shrunken red blood cells cannot carry their full capacity of oxygen to the tissues.

The imbalance of sodium in fresh water drowning is the opposite to that of salt water. Water enters the lungs and is drawn through the membranes of the alveoli into the blood. This occurs because sodium content of the blood is higher than that of fresh water. In extreme cases, where fresh water has very little sodium, water can be drawn in over several minutes so that the blood volume of a victim doubles. This blood dilution causes severe chemical imbalances, resulting in irregularities in the body functions. An imbalance of electrolytes in the blood is caused by the dilution, and this contributes to ventricular fibrillation in 80% of the freshwater drowning cases.

As red blood cells fill up with water, another problem arises. In some cases when the water content of the red blood cells becomes too great, the cell will explode (hemolysis) and will no longer be able to carry oxygen. If enough red blood cells suffer hemolysis, oxygen transportation is significantly reduced.

Whether a drowned body will float or sink depends on the amount of water taken into the lungs and stomach and on the victim's original buoyancy. Positively buoyant victims will float; negatively buoyant victims will sink. However, if the victim was borderline buoyant or non-buoyant, vital capacity may change the body's ability to float. As the body descends to a greater depth, the lungs are squeezed of their residual volume, the air that keeps the lungs inflated. Bubbles may surface from the victim for quite some time. Most bodies eventually surface if they are not held down in some way. The surfacing is caused by the development of carbon dioxide and other gases that are created as the body decays. Cold water slows the decaying process.

Special Problems Associated With Potential Accidents

Although aquatic environments provide numerous opportunities for fun and relaxation, certain situations could cause potential accidents if these situations are not understood and avoided.

Hyperventilation

Hyperventilation, or overventilation as it occurs in an aquatic sense, is performed by inhaling and exhaling deeply and rapidly in order to stay underwater longer. Hyperventilation does increase the time you can spend underwater; however, it is dangerous because you risk the possibility of passing out. Underwater swimming is a valuable skill, enabling a lifeguard to surface dive and swim under the surface of the water to search for or rescue a drowned victim. In this case hyperventilating three to six times before diving is a risk, but may be necessary.

When you hyperventilate, the following occurs: (a) The deep breaths lower the percentage of carbon dioxide (CO_2) in the residual volume of air in the lungs, and (b) the carbon dioxide level in the blood triggers the breathing center, the medulla oblongata, to take a breath. When the carbon dioxide level is lowered, you can remain underwater longer because you delay reaching the trigger point. The danger occurs at the carbon dioxide trigger point because the blown-off CO_2 is set above the anoxic point. The anoxic point is the point at which the lack of oxygen is so severe that you become unconscious (black out). Normally, the percentage of oxygen and carbon dioxide in the residual volume is set so that when you hold your breath, the carbon dioxide trigger will always be reached before the anoxia point.

Hyperventilating lowers the percent level of carbon dioxide so that you reach the anoxic level before ever reaching the carbon dioxide trigger point and that urge to breath. The important thing to remember is that by hyperventilating, the actual oxygen increase is small compared to the deadly consequence of dropping the carbon dioxide level to below the anoxic point.

Reports show that the onset of unconsciousness is like falling asleep—a person really does not notice it. In some cases, the swimmer has been known to continue swimming underwater for some distance even after becoming unconscious. In other cases, there is a euphoric feeling that the swimmer could stay underwater forever. Kicking may also continue but slows until the victim begins to surface and swallows water.

Overinflating the lungs usually causes an early feeling of the need to breathe. This may be overcome by exhaling some air so that the chest returns to a normally expanded position.

Overexertion, pressure effect, and positional effect are the three other situations that can result in a blackout during underwater swimming:

- *Overexertion.* During overexertion the body will utilize the stored oxygen very quickly. This rapid use brings about anoxia much more quickly. Poorly conditioned, overaged, or overtaxed swimmers are especially susceptible to anoxia caused by overexertion, and this is a major concern to the lifeguard. Overexertion also decreases the sensitivity of the CO_2 trigger.
- *Pressure effect.* When diving 20 ft or more, which is quite unusual for most lifeguards, the increased pressure of deeper water causes increased oxygen use. Upon surfacing, the lifeguard may become anoxic and black out.
- *Positional effect.* On extended shallow underwater swims, the oxygen level will drop, causing hypoxia—however, not to the point where the partial pressure is inadequate for supplying oxygen to the brain, but far enough so that when the swimmer stands up, enough blood will leave the brain. The oxygen supply to the brain is thus reduced to the possible point of anoxia, causing the swimmer to become unconscious.

Ear Squeeze

Ear squeeze is the pain you feel in your eardrum due to the increase in pressure when diving into water 10 ft and deeper. When you dive to 10 ft or more, the increased water pressure is greater in the outer ear than it is in the middle ear, causing the tympanic membrane to stretch and cause pain. The pain occurs because the middle ear pressure remains at its normal surface pressure of 14.7 psi (pounds/square inch), while the water pressure on the outer ear and eardrum is much greater. To alleviate this problem, pinch off your nose, keep your mouth closed, and attempt to gently blow out. This action increases the pressure in the throat, which opens the eustachian tube that connects the throat and middle ear. This procedure increases pressure in the middle ear that equalizes pressure with the outer ear and allows the tympanic membrane to return to its usual position, stopping the pain.

You should equalize the pressure every 5 ft to be safe and avoid possible injury to the tympanic membrane. Increasing the pressure without equalizing it could puncture or pierce the membrane and cause a ruptured eardrum. It is not safe to swim with a ruptured eardrum until it is fully healed. Likewise, it is not safe to swim underwater with a cold or flu because the eustachian tubes become clogged and will not allow air to pass through as you try to equalize pressure.

Cramps

The actual process of how cramps occur is not fully understood. Cramps can be triggered by the lack of salt, calcium, potassium, dehydration or oxygen. The lack of oxygen to the muscle is one of the most accepted theories of the cause of swimming cramps. As a result of this lack of oxygen, lactic acid builds up and causes the muscle to contract beyond its range. When a sufficient amount of lactic acid has accumulated, the muscle contracts beyond its normal range, resulting in the knotting of the muscle and the pain. This condition of the muscle is called contracture.

In the 1930s through the 1950s, cramps were blamed as the major cause of drowning. However, they are non-life-threatening if the victim keeps from panicking. When a cramp strikes, panic may cause drowning. If swimmers are informed on how to handle this situation, panic could be avoided. Most cramps occur in the calf, foot, and hand because these are the most active body parts while swimming. In addition, these parts are the farthest away from the heart and therefore receive oxygenated blood last.

Immersion Hypothermia

The word *hypo* means "low." The word *thermia* refers to temperature. *Immersion* means "submerged in water." Basically, then, *hypothermia* is low body temperature due to immersion in cold water. Water cools the body 25 to 27 times faster than does air. Even in water with a temperature of 72° to 78°, unconsciousness can occur within 3 to 12 hours. In very cold water, your extremities (arms and legs) cool rapidly, but it takes 10 to 15 min before the temperature of your heart, brain, and internal organs begin to lose heat. It is not a good idea to disrobe or inflate your clothing in cold water because they act to protect your body from heat loss. Disrobe and inflate your clothes only in warm (80°) water. Usually upon immersion in cold water, your initial reaction is an uncontrolled reflexive gasp and uncontrolled hyperventilation, which indicates a lack of control of breathing. If you try to put your head underwater, you will find it difficult to hold your breath and will experience a very painful explosive feeling between the eyes.

The cold water immediately causes peripheral vasoconstriction (tightening) of the blood vessels, which makes the blood vessels close to the skin narrower, causing the skin to turn white. The lack of blood flow to the fingers causes them to lose the ability to grip. The coldness and lack of blood eventually affects the control and coordination of the larger muscles. Confusion and foggy thinking is also evident.

The human body reacts to protect itself by creating more heat: The pulse increases and shivering begins. Shivering is one way the body creates more heat. Shivering can create three to five times more heat than if the muscles are resting. However, for those people who have heart problems, extra shivering and increased pulse could cause additional problems. Research done by the U.S. Coast Guard and from the University of Victoria, British Columbia, (1977) has shown the following:

- Adipose tissue (fat) is an insulator and decreases heat loss.

- Unlike still water, moving water hastens body heat loss.
- Shock and hysteria can occur upon immersion in very cold water.
- Clothing will help prevent heat loss.
- Wearing PFDs increases survival time.
- Even with a PFD, the body loses heat 35% faster when moving compared to floating still. At 50° a good swimmer can swim no more than ¾ of a mile before becoming exhausted. *Do not attempt to swim* unless it is to reach a nearby craft, a fellow survivor, or a floating object that can give you support.
- Survival floating (drownproofing) creates an 82% greater heat loss as compared to floating with a PFD.

A positive mental attitude and the will to survive are important in helping prolong survival time. The chart shown in Table 3.2 was developed by the U.S. Coast Guard (1977) based on research into the effects of cold water on the human body.

Table 3.2   Effects of Cold Water on the Human Body*

Water Temperature	Expected Survival Time
28°	15 min
32°	15-30 min
40°	30-90 min
50°	1-4 hr
60°	2-24 hr
70°	3-40 hr
80°	Indefinite

*Adapted from the U.S. Coast Guard (1977).

Studies have shown that the body has four major heat loss areas. These areas are (a) the eyes and forehead, (b) the front of the neck (carotid arteries), (c) the front sides of the rib cage, including the armpits, and (d) the crease between the trunk (torso) and upper legs (femoral arteries). These studies prompted the development of the heat escape lessening posture (HELP), which is discussed further in chapter 2, "Personal Safety." The HELP position increases survival time as indicated in Table 3.3.

Table 3.3   Survival Time Under Various Conditions*

Conditions	Water Temperature	Estimated Survival Time in Hours
No PFD		
Drownproofing	40°	1 hr 5 min
	50°	1 hr 26 min
	60°	2 hr 12 min
Treading	40°	1 hr 24 min
	50°	1 hr 58 min
	60°	3 hr 4 min
PFD		
No HELP	40°	1 hr 58 min
	50°	2 hr 37 min
	60°	4 hr 7 min
HELP	40°	2 hr 52 min
	50°	3 hr 30 min
	60°	5 hr 58 min

*Adapted from the U.S. Coast Guard (1980) and Canadian Red Cross (1983).

As you can see, the HELP position provided the greatest survival times, followed by simply wearing a PFD. When groups of people (three to four) are in a cold water immersion situation, they may get into a huddled position, drawing themselves to each other, to ensure that the heat loss areas are covered.

Children are more susceptible to heat loss in immersion situations because of their small size and the close proximity of major arteries to the skin. The child should be removed from the water if at all possible. If it is not possible, then sandwiching the child between a group of three to four huddling adults will help. The body heat generated by the group should cause the water in the area between them to be slightly warmer. This may be a difficult position to maintain and will probably take practice.

Emergency treatment.   Do not delay treatment because hypothermia can cause complications even after the victim is out of the water. Table 3.4 is a compilation of several charts indicating levels of internal core temperature and their corresponding signs and symptoms.

Table 3.4   Levels of Hypothermia and Their Signs and Symptoms*

Level	Core Temperature	Signs and Symptoms
	98.6°	Normal core temperature.
Mild	94°-95°	Conscious and alert, but hyperventilating; vigorous and uncontrolled shivering.
Moderate	90°-93°	Conscious, foggy thinking; speech impairment; reasoning ability lowered; loss of use of the hands to grasp, clumsy.
Severe	86°-90°	Maybe unconscious; mental ability severely impaired; muscle rigidity; skin may become cyanotic (blue); very cold to the touch; cardiac arrythmias (uneven pulse) occurs.
Very severe	81°-85°	Usually unconscious; muscular rigidity persists; slowing of respirations and pulse.
Critical	Below 80°	Unconscious; reflexes gone; breathing shallow or undetectable; cardiac arrhythmias causing cardiac arrest.

*Adapted from the U.S. Coast Guard (1977) and Canadian Red Cross (1983).

When a thermometer is not available, the following signs will help identify the hypothermic victim:

1. *Respiration.* Breathing is usually slow and labored. Initially however, the respiration rate is very high.
2. *Pulse.* The pulse is usually slow and irregular. Initially, however, the pulse rate will be very high.
3. *Consciousness.* By comparing the victim's level of consciousness and condition with the signs and symptoms listed in Table 3.4, the lifeguard can approximate the body temperatures.
4. *Skin color.* Cyanosis (blueness) will be evident, especially in the lips and in the fingernail beds.
5. *Pupils.* The pupils of the eyes are generally constricted and react poorly to light.

Cold water drowning. Amazing stories of recovery from 30- to 45-min submersions in cold water have been in the headlines since the late 70s. This is due primarily to work done by Nemiroff of the U.S. Coast Guard and Conn from Canada. The latest information available to lifeguards is that if someone drowns, even if all signs of life are absent, CPR must be started and continued until the victim reaches an emergency care facility. This is particularly true in cold water drowning because these victims, many of whom have fallen through the ice (especially children), have been known to be under the surface from 15 to 45 min, and, after 4 to 5 hours of CPR and definitive therapy provided by knowledgeable physicians, have regained pulse and respirations. The more amazing part of the story is that in many cases little or no brain damage occurs.

The mammalian diving reflex is thought to take place in water that is 70° and below. The effects are much greater the colder the water. Basically, the body goes into a form of hibernation. The cold water causes vasoconstriction in the blood vessels of the arms and legs. The coldness also causes a slowing and in some cases a stoppage of the metabolic activity at the cellular level in the tissues of the arms and legs. The low metabolic activity, coupled with peripheral vasoconstriction, partially eliminates the delivery of oxygen to the limbs because of the restricted blood flow. This allows more available blood flow and thus more oxygen to be used solely for the vital organs.

As the temperature of the major body organs drops, metabolic activity and oxygen utilization of the heart, lungs, brain, and kidneys are reduced. Surgeons cool body organs during operations so that the organs do not suffer cell damage due to a lack of oxygen. This same idea is carried out naturally in cases of cold water submersion.

With this total reduction of oxygenation and the cool internal temperatures, the heart, lungs, kidney, and brain seem to be able to survive with the oxygen in the organ and in the surrounding tissues and blood. In this situation, you must begin CPR as soon as the victim is removed from the water. Then call the ambulance to have the victim transported to an emergency care facility. Immediate transportation is mandatory so that rewarming and resuscitation can be continued and administered effectively under the physician's supervision.

As in hypothermia, the basic premise is that the internal core must be rewarmed first. If available, warm (104°), humidified oxygen should be used during resuscitation, or the torso of the victim should be immersed into a warm bath, ensuring that the arms and legs are kept out. If the victim is rewarmed as a whole, the arms and legs will thaw first, drawing large amounts of blood away from the internal core due to increased metabolic activity. This may cause severe shock (blood loss) to the internal core, resulting in death.

An additional problem encountered when rewarming the body is that cold blood from the limbs flows back into the internal core, continuing to cause the internal core temperature to drop. This is called the after-drop syndrome. After-drop is held to a minimum if the victim remains still and if the peripheral body parts are not rewarmed.

Review Questions

1. Name three things that signal a shift in the weather.
2. Why is swimming in water currents potentially dangerous?
3. How would you swim out of a strong current?
4. Do underwater plants and weeds pose a potential danger?
5. If you get tangled in underwater grass, how should you get free?
6. What potential hazards do wave pools pose versus traditional swimming pools?
7. If your specific gravity is 1.5, will you sink or float?
8. Why do you float easier in salt water than in fresh water?
9. If your specific gravity is slightly greater than 1.0, what other factor will influence whether you sink or float?
10. Briefly discuss the stages of drowning.
11. Why is it important to give CPR to a victim who has been submerged in cold water for 10 minutes?
12. What is the mammalian diving reflex?

chapter 4

AQUATIC RESCUES

No matter how proficient a lifeguard you are and no matter how many accidents you prevent, you have to be prepared for the time when an accident could happen and a swimming rescue is your best or only option. Your ability to identify the emergency, to analyze the options, to make a decision, and to effect a rescue will determine whether or not you are successful. As a professional lifeguard, you may act alone or as a member of a team. Furthermore, because you have practiced the procedures for a rescue situation many times in training, much of the stress associated with decision making is reduced, allowing you to analyze the options in a more relaxed state. The actions that must be taken to effect a rescue in an aquatic emergency are outlined in Figure 4.1. Each action will be discussed in detail in this chapter.

Victim Identification

The first step in executing an effective rescue is obviously to detect the need for action. As a trained professional, you can reduce the anxiety of identification by learning to look for potential victims and by analyzing options before the potential accidents occur. By doing this, you can determine what option is best for you. Comparing size, swimming proficiency, and the comfort of potential victims in the water can help you determine in advance a course of action effective for your own size and skill. In some situations you might only need to use a simple nonswimming (throwing or reaching) rescue or swimming assist. However, if you wait until the victim panics, you and the victim will be faced with considerably more danger. Making these decisions *early* is the key to determining the need for action.

Scanning

Another way to detect a potential emergency is in the way you scan your area. Make sure you cover your area, glancing in a sweeping motion constantly. Look at facial expressions. Divide your scanning time unequally—the danger areas should take priority over the other areas. Make sure people come up from their dives. Stay in eye contact with your other guards, but don't turn your back on your area. Develop a regular rotation system to reduce fatigue and to prevent bore-

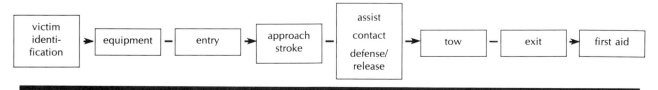

4.1 Lifesaving flowchart

dom while on duty. Keep in mind that accidents are likely to happen in some areas more than in others. Review the chart on pages 90-91 in chapter 7 and define those areas in your own pool or environment.

Guidelines for Early Detection

Because you will be called on daily to make decisions regarding aquatic emergencies, establish guidelines to help identify potential victims. There are two basic categories: one before swimmers get into the water; the other after swimmers get into the water. In both cases, check for the following:

Before entering water:
- Age extremes—either the very young or the very old
- Weight extremes—either very heavy or very thin
- Pale or white individuals—possibly show a lack of exposure or experience outdoors
- Unstable or intoxicated individuals—impaired movement and behavior patterns
- Flotation users—for support or for relaxation
- Physical impairment—limited ability around the water

While in the water:
- Weak stroke and kick—lack of competent ability
- Hair in eyes—person possibly too concerned with keeping head above the water to push hair out of eyes
- Glassy, empty, anxious-looking eyes—facial expression prior to exhaustion
- Two heads together—sign of double drowning
- Hand waving—a sign of needing help
- Swimmer moving toward rocks or piers—swimmer caught in a current
- Erratic behavior—anything out of the ordinary
- Clinging to objects for security—too tired to swim to safety

Being able to identify potential aquatic emergencies is crucial for a lifeguard; however, it doesn't mean you should be excessively tense. This extreme could lead to some embarrassing situations if you overreact to a would-be emergency. In some ways being overprepared is as damaging as not being prepared at all. Stay relaxed. Keep a vigilant watch over your area, but let your common sense keep your responsibility in perspective. Once you've determined the need for a rescue, maintain eye contact with the victim until you have completed the rescue.

Rescue Equipment

Rescue equipment is one of the lifeguard's most valuable tools. To a lifeguard, making a rescue without equipment is like playing football without a helmet or catching a ball without a glove. It can be done, but why make a rescue more dangerous than it already is? Sometimes, however, rescue equipment will not be available; regardless, you must still be able to complete the rescue. Make it a habit, however, to practice with your equipment. Consider it a natural part of your uniform and don't leave your stand without it!

Different facilities and aquatic environments call for different kinds of rescues. For a pool, a rescue might take a matter of seconds and involve a minimal amount of swimming, whereas in a lake or surf environment, you might have to swim for a few minutes to get to the victim. *Rescue equipment aids and reduces the risk of harm to you and victim.*

Shepherd's Crook or Reaching Pole

The shepherd's crook and reaching pole are lightweight wood, aluminum, or fiberglass rods about 10 to 15 ft long. The shepherd's crook has a blunt hook on one end that is large enough to place around an unconscious victim. Both the shepherd's crook and pole can be used to reach a conscious victim (see Figure 4.2).

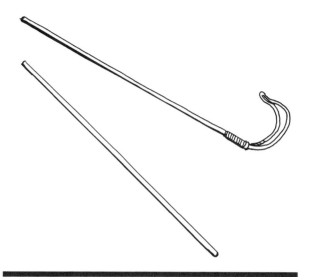

4.2 Shepherd's crook and reaching pole

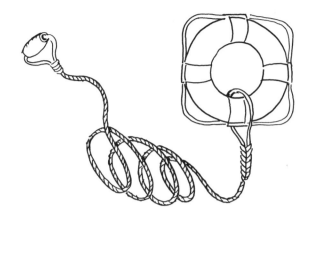

4.3 Ring buoy

Ring Buoy

A ring buoy, pictured in Figure 4.3, is made of lightweight buoyant material, weighing usually no more than 2½ lb, and is used primarily on lake fronts and around pools. As a tool for a lifeguard, the ring buoy has a 40 to 50 ft ¼ in. line attached, with a buoyant attachment or wrist loop at one end to accommodate throwing assists. The ring buoy is generally only effective on a distressed swimmer. As you throw the ring buoy, secure the knot under your stable foot or slip the loop around your nonthrowing wrist. Aim slightly beyond the victim, maintaining voice and eye contact with the victim and buoy. Once the victim has grabbed the buoy, pull the victim to safety.

If the victim becomes too tired to hold on and more than one lifeguard is present, one guard can throw the buoy while another swims to assist. In this case, both the guard and the victim are pulled to safety. If you are alone and your victim cannot grasp the buoy or if your throw misses its target, swim to the victim and hand him or her the buoy, being careful to keep it between yourself and the victim. Recoiling the rope and throwing the buoy again is *not* recommended for

lifeguards who have the ability to make a swimming assist primarily because of the lost time and the possibility that your second throw will also miss the victim's grasp. *Lifesavers*, however, should throw the ring buoy a second time as described in chapter 2 to avoid having to enter the water.

Rescue Tube

A rescue tube (see Figure 4.4) is a 3 ft x 6 ft x 40 in. buoyant object made of a soft molded foam. It has a 6-ft line with a loop attached to one end for easy towing when the guard puts it over his or her head and shoulder. It is a versa-

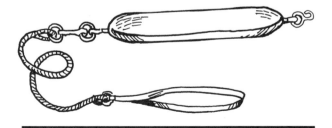

4.4 Rescue tube

tile aid and can be used for (a) reaching to a struggling victim to avoid contact until the victim regains composure, (b) towing a passive/unconscious victim, or (c) supporting the rescuer in certain situations.

When you enter the water, keep the tube to the side of your body. As you approach the victim, do a quick reverse and place the tube around the victim in one of the two following ways: Submerge the tube (by grabbing it in the middle) as you turn the victim to a face-up position, and attach the ends in back (see Figure 4.5); or take both ends of the tube in your hands and reach around the victim (from the back), as in Figure 4.6, attaching the ends as you turn the victim to a face-up position. In some situations it may be easier to attach the tube around yourself in order to tow most efficiently. Please note that in the event that the victim should be submerged before you reach him or her, release your equipment before you dive underwater.

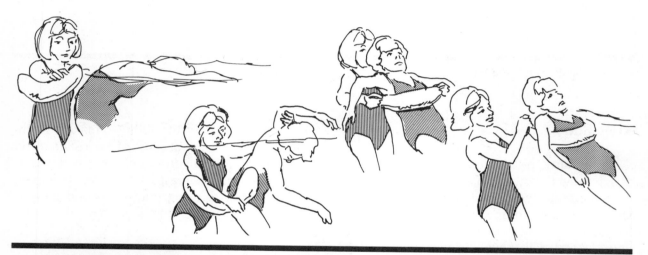

4.5   Attaching the rescue tube in back of the victim

4.6   Attaching the rescue tube in front of the victim

Rescue Can or Buoy

The rescue can, illustrated in Figure 4.7, is made of a lightweight, hard plastic, and buoyant material with molded handles along the sides and end. Similar to the rescue tube, it also has a tow rope attached to one end. Its bright color and lightness make it a versatile tool for the lifeguard. It can be used as a defensive aid to avoid contact with the victim or as a buoyancy aid for active and passive victims. The rescue can is also useful in team rescues, in swimming and non-swimming rescues or assists, and in all aquatic environments. However, it cannot be used to support an unconscious victim without a lifeguard maintaining contact and there is a possibility that a tired swimmer could lose his or her grip on the handles if tired.

If the victim is conscious, swim out to the victim, maintaining eye contact. As you approach, do a quick reverse, reach back and pull the trailing buoy into grasp. Keep the buoy between you and the victim. Encourage the victim to grab hold (see Figure 4.8); then talk to and reassure the victim. At this point you can determine the best option for reaching safety. For an unconscious victim, the rescue can will probably be of greatest use to you for buoyancy because there is no way to attach it around the victim independently.

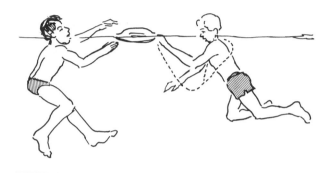

4.8 Reaching assist with a rescue can

Rescue Board

A rescue board is similar to a surf board but provides more support and is slightly larger. Shown in Figure 4.9, the rescue board is about 10 ft long and 22 in. wide, and made of wood, fiberglass, or foam.

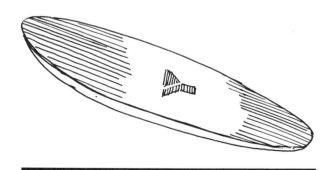

4.9 Rescue board

4.7 Rescue can

For an unconscious victim, use the rescue board as follows:

1. Paddle to the victim, turn the victim's back to the board, and reach over victim's shoulders to armpits.
2. Kneel on the board and slowly lean back, slowly flipping the board until the victim is lying across the back of the board.
3. Position the victim straight on the board and paddle to safety. (If you have a rescue board that has a fin on the bottom like a surfboard, you may need to flip the board first before you contact the victim.)
4. From your paddling position, approach the victim. With the speed of the board assisting, grab the wrist and flip the victim across the board in front of you and paddle to safety.

Balance is important in this maneuver to avoid losing contact with the board in the process.

For a conscious victim, proceed as follows:

1. Approach the victim, slide off the board opposite the victim, and grab and pull the victim's wrist over the top of the board to the other side.
2. Flip board over, pulling the top part of the victim across the board.
3. Slide victim's feet and head into proper position on board as illustrated in Figure 4.10.
4. To transport the victim, slide onto the board behind the victim (victim is face down on the board) and between the legs. You may have some of your weight over the victim's back to establish a secure position. From this position, paddle to safety.

You can use the surfboard in an assist that uses the same lifesaving skill as a tired swimmer's assist, except that it is done with the swimmer holding the board instead of your shoulders. Approach the swimmer and ask if he or she needs help; ask the swimmer to relax and hold the end of the board. Explain that if he or she keeps the arms straight and leans back, you will be able to paddle him or her back to shore (see Figure 4.11). As in all equipment rescues, practice with the equipment until you become comfortable using it.

4.10   Flipping the rescue board to secure a conscious victim

4.11   Using the rescue board to help a tired swimmer

Mask, Fins, and Snorkel

The mask, fins, and snorkel are special pieces of rescue equipment with which you should practice and be familar. They are especially useful in searching for submerged victims or divers where the water visibility is limited. Check the mask (illustrated in Figure 4.12) for proper fit by putting it over your eyes and nose without the strap and inhaling through your nose. The mask should stay in place. In the water, clear your mask of water by pressing against the top of the mask and exhaling through your nose. This should force the water out.

Fins, shown in Figure 4.12, will extend the power and strength of your kick. Make sure they fit comfortably. Kick naturally, slightly exaggerating the waving motion of your legs. Fins will allow you to cover more distance faster when searching for a submerged victim.

Your snorkel should be attached to your mask strap to ensure proper positioning when you surface and try to clear it (see Figure 4.12). As you go underwater, water will fill the snorkel. Be careful not to breathe in. To clear the snorkel, blow out forcefully as the snorkel breaks the surface.

Keep the equipment clean after each use by cleansing it in fresh water, occasionally in soapy water. Make sure the equipment is dry before it is stored, and keep it out of sunlight and heat for extended periods of time. Becoming proficient at using this equipment will take practice; becoming skilled will take additional training.

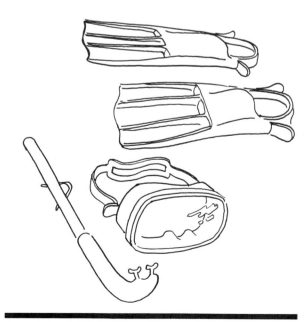

4.12   Mask, fins, and snorkel

Swimming Rescues

In the event that you do not have any equipment available, and a swimming rescue is the last resort, keep in mind that the emotional state of the victim, the distance to the victim, and the aquatic environment will help you determine the appropriate course of action.

Water Entries

The first physical step involved in a swimming rescue is entering the water. Of the different methods, the lifeguard will have to determine what is most appropriate in a particular set of circumstances; whatever method is used, always maintain eye contact and communicate with the victim.

Stride jump.   In water over 7 ft deep, you can quickly enter and maintain eye contact with the victim using a stride jump. As you leave the wall, lean forward and step out, stretching one leg in front, arms out, slightly back, and above your shoulders. As your body enters the water, force your legs together, like doing a scissors kick. Bring your arms forward or down as they go under; this will slow down the jump and keep your head above the water. The stride jump is illustrated in Figure 4.13.

4.13   Stride jump

Compact jump.   To enter water from a height of 5 ft or more, use a compact jump for safety. As you jump, place one hand over your mouth and chin, holding your nose. Cross the other arm across the chest over the first arm. Maintain a relatively straight body position. (Leaning forward or backward slightly could cause a back, head, or chest injury.) As you contact the water, bend the knees slightly to absorb the shock. Depending on the bottom, push off diagonally and head for the victim. Keep in mind that you will lose eye contact with the victim as you go under. Remember where you last saw the victim so you can proceed from there if for some reason you cannot locate him or her immediately when you surface.

Shallow dive.   When time and speed are crucial, a shallow dive might be the most appropriate entry. Check for the water depth before doing any dive. In addition to the water depth, make sure you check the water conditions. Seaweed and pollution might make a shallow dive undesirable and inappropriate. Execute a shallow dive similar to the way you would do a racing dive (see Figure 4.14). As you enter the water,

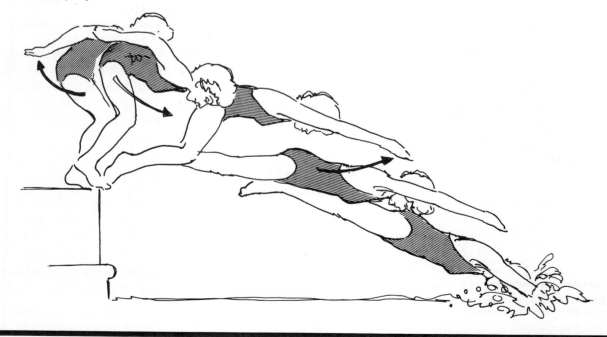

4.14   Shallow dive

immediately aim or steer up with your arms and head and begin swimming to the victim. Maintain eye contact.

Surf entry.   From a sloping shoreline, run into the water using high-stepping strides. Begin swimming toward the victim as soon as possible. In a surf situation, a shallow dive, as shown in Figure 4.15, may be used to get through the breaking waves. In a heavy surf, it may take several dives to get through the breakers.

Approach Stroke

After you enter the water, you have to get to the victim as soon as possible. Here, time is the enemy. The distance to be covered and the condition of the victim will help you determine which stroke to use. Your primary goal is the safety of the victim, and the sooner you arrive, the more you will minimize the chance of harm to that victim. Always keep eye contact with the victim. You must arrive with enough energy to make the rescue and to tow the victim back.

Approach crawl.   The approach crawl is an adapatation of the front crawl stroke: You keep your head above the water and your eye on the victim. This stroke moves you through the water quickly and is appropriate for short distances.

Approach breaststroke.   This stroke is an adaptation of the breaststroke. Keep your head above water throughout the shortened strokes and your eye on the victim. For longer distances, this stroke may help you conserve energy.

Quick Reverse

As you approach a conscious victim, regardless of whether they are active or passive, you should execute a maneuver referred to as a quick reverse when you are just out of the victim's arm range. Depending on your approach stroke, you will need to reverse your direction by leaning backward, turning 90°, bringing your legs to your chest, and extending them between you and your victim while sculling. Talk to the victim. Emphasize that you are there to help. If the victim is below the surface, to save time you may decide not to use the quick reverse and immediately contact the victim. Assess the situation carefully as you approach the victim: A seemingly passive victim could become active when you get close.

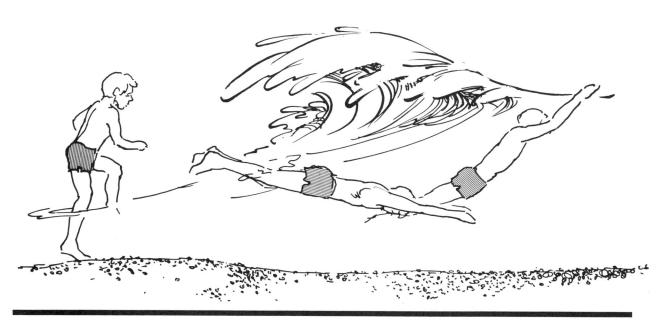

4.15 Surf entry

Surface Dives

If the victim is submerged, a surface dive is probably the quickest way to reach him or her if you have to dive for any distance. The length of time the victim has been submerged and the water conditions will be factors in determining which type of surface dive you should use. With a submerged victim, time and speed are crucial.

Feet-first surface dive. If the water is murky and you are not sure what's on the bottom or the depth of the water, a feet-first surface dive will allow you to go under safely in a vertical position. From a treading water position, take one large kick, snapping your legs together, and bring your arms to your sides. This should push you up in the water, and gravity will cause you to move downward. Keep your body streamlined and as your movement slows, lift your arms (palms up) from your sides to over your head (see Figure 4.16). This should increase your downward motion. From this point, you may have to roll forward and reach downward and kick to keep going down.

Head-first surface dive. As you approach the place where the victim submerged, a head-first surface dive will allow you to dive accurately downward to the victim. Swimming into the surface dive will give you more momentum into the downward motion. From a prone position, reach forward, tuck your chin, and bend at the waist. As the arms and upper body pull downward, the hips and lower body lift and the legs extend upward out of the water from a pike position (as shown in Figure 4.17). This gives your body momentum downward.

Depending on your ability and strength, you may choose to do the head-first surface dive from either a tuck or pike position. In a tucked head-first surface dive, as the arms and upper body bend forward and reach downward, the legs pull up to a tuck, then extend upward (see Figure 4.17). By shortening the radius between your hip and feet (tuck action), it is a little easier to keep your hips closer to the surface; then your extension upward will push more of your leg length upward out of the water, resulting in a stronger vertical dive.

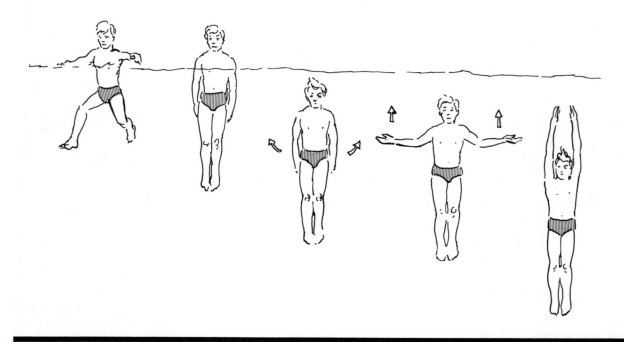

4.16   Feet first surface dive

(a)

(b)

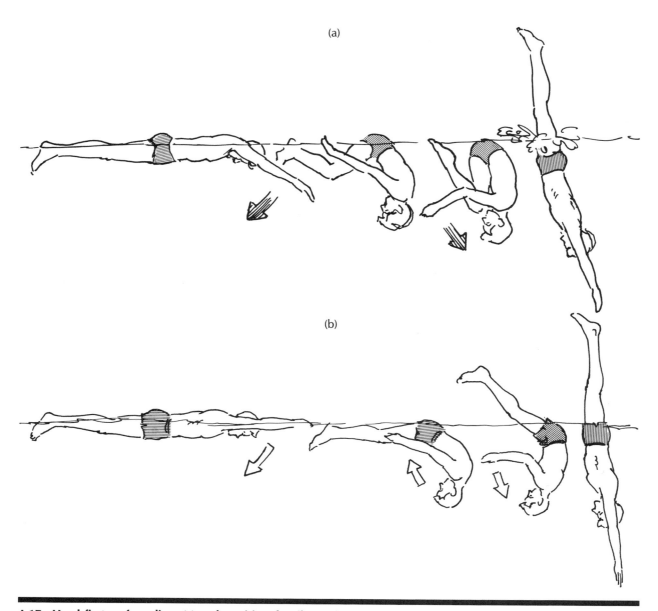

4.17   Head first surface dives (a) tuck position (b) pike position

Swimming Assists

As an alert guard, you will hopefully be able to detect an emergency before it happens. In many situations swimmers may not be sure of their limitations, or for other reasons may become fatigued. Regardless of the reason, some swimmers may need assistance rather than an actual rescue. As you approach the tired swimmer, communicate with him or her. Ask if he or she needs help. Reassure the swimmer throughout the assist. Explain what you are doing and what you want him or her to do. Keep your instructions clear, simple, and positive.

Front assist.   As you approach the victim from the front, do a quick reverse and ask, "Do you need help?" If the victim says yes, swim to the side and behind the victim. If the victim follows you, persuade him or her to continue to face toward shore. If you are swimming to the left side, grab the victim's left upper arm from underneath with your right hand—your fingers in and thumb outside. Grasp the arm as close to the armpit as possible (see Figure 4.18). Encourage the victim to remain calm as you grab the arm. Remain slightly behind and to the side the the victim to avoid the possibility of him or her grabbing you. Use the whip kick or inverted scissors kick to move the victim and yourself to shore or to the edge of the pool. Avoid dragging the victim in unless his or her condition deteriorates and he or she needs to be towed.

4.18   Front assist

Rear assist.   To use this assist, your victim must be in a back-float position. Approach the distressed swimmer and ask if he or she needs help. Assist by reaching from behind under the armpit. Reach with right hand to the right armpit, left hand to left armpit, as shown in Figure 4.19. Constantly reassure the victim and encourage the swimmer to relax and keep the head and ears

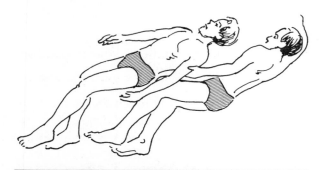

4.19   Rear assist

in the water. Use a sidestroke or inverted breaststroke kick to swim directly behind the swimmer.

Tired swimmer's assist.   If the tired swimmer is calm and cooperative, this assist is effective. As you approach the tired swimmer, do a quick reverse and ask, "Do you need help?" If the victim says yes, approach him or her slowly with a breaststroke. This assist should only be used on a tired swimmer, not on a distressed swimmer. A distressed swimmer is in an emotional state beyond tired and is more prone to panic. Ask the swimmer to lie back into a back-float position and place his or her hands on your shoulders with the thumbs pointing down to prevent them from sliding. Continue to swim forward, causing the swimmer to move to a horizontal position (see Figure 4.20). Continue

4.20   Tired swimmer assist

to encourage the victim to keep his or her head back, arms straight, and to allow the legs to part. By putting the head back, the victim will float higher in the water. Keeping the elbows straight will prevent the victim from running up onto you. Spreading the victim's legs will give you the appropriate chest and kicking room.

Contact

As you get closer to the victim before actual contact, assess the situation and the condition of the victim. The process of contacting a victim includes parts of the rescue that result in either an assist, a defense, or a release, and ends with a tow. The condition of the victim will determine what course of action is most appropriate. In most aquatic emergencies in which a swimming rescue is necessary, the victim is in either a passive or active state.

Passive and active victims.   A *passive* victim is unconscious and not displaying any active movements. Most of the time, these victims are found face down or submerged in the water. Rescue of these individuals is critical if there is hope for their survival. An *active* victim is thrashing or showing signs of panic and extreme fear. These individuals are more dangerous to rescue without risking harm to yourself. However, active victims can become passive victims easily if allowed to thrash around too much.

Leveling.   Upon contact with every passive or active victim, you must level the victim from a vertical position in the water to a horizontal one for easier towing. With passive victims you can make the initial contact and then kick vigorously

1 or 2 body lengths to move the victim to a horizontal position before securing the tow.

With the active victim it may be very dangerous to level in the standard way. Once contact is made with the active victim, you must immediately secure a control tow (see pp. 49-50). Both hands are in use so you must kick vigorously to begin the leveling process. A hand, leg or hip lift will speed the leveling process. Place either your hand, leg, or hip against the victim's back and buttocks and push. This will move the victim from vertical to horizontal and will make towing easier. The leveling process is illustrated in Figure 4.21.

Rear passive armpit contact.   Approach the passive victim who is face down in the water from the rear, do a quick reverse about an arm's length away, and ask if he or she needs help. If there is no response, move in immediately. Grab the victim's right arm close to the armpit with your right hand, with your fingers in toward the victim's chest and your thumb toward the back.

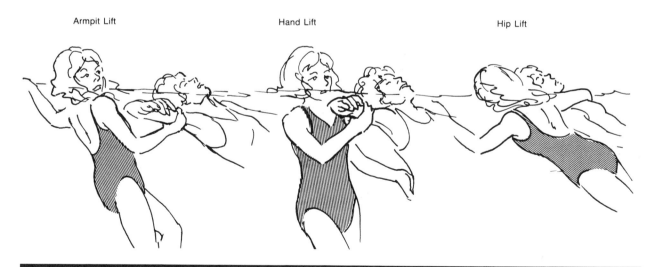

Armpit Lift   Hand Lift   Hip Lift

4.21   Leveling the victim using the armpit lift, hand lift, and hip lift

4.22   Rear passive arm contact

Depending on the size of the victim, it may be necessary to use one of the lifts to get the victim into a horizontal position. Kick hard to level and move into the appropriate tow (see Figure 4.22).

Rear passive chin contact.   Approach the passive victim from the rear. Do a quick reverse and reach over the victim's shoulder. Be careful to grab the victim's chin, not the throat area. Level the victim by pulling the chin back and by putting pressure on the victim's shoulder for leverage,

as illustrated in Figure 4.23. Move into the appropriate tow. This contact allows a limited time for the control of the victim. It is important to use this on an unconscious victim only: Level and move into a tow quickly.

Rear active cross-chest contact.   With an active victim, approach from the rear. You must approach the victim swiftly but cautiously and be ready to escape if the victim turns toward you. Use the momentum of your stroke to maintain

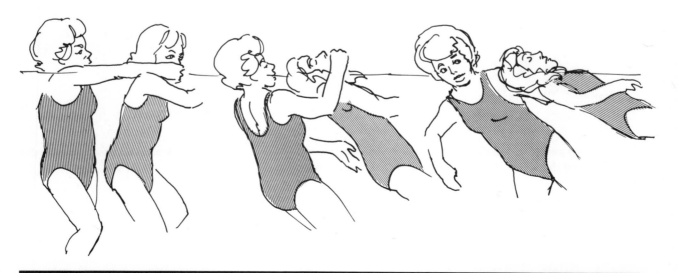

4.23   Rear passive chin contact

control of the situation. As you contact the victim, do a quick reverse, apply an armpit lift with your right hand (fingers in, thumbs out) while reaching with the left arm over the victim's shoulder in a cross-chest control tow as shown in Figure 4.24 and described on pages 49-50. Prior to securing a cross-chest contact on an active victim, it is important to use an armpit lift to get him or her in a better position for towing. Generally, if the cross-chest were applied by itself on an active victim, the victim would ride too low. Your initial contact causes the victim's shoulder to sink 3 to 4 in. By the time the hand is securely in place for the cross-chest, towing would be awkward because of the victim's low position. The armpit lift ensures a tight cross-chest control tow. The armpit lift itself is not a safe tow for an active victim. The cross-chest control must follow the armpit level immediately after the lift.

Front passive upper arm contact. Approach the passive victim lying face down from the front. Reverse momentum about an arm's length from the victim. Splash the victim and ask if he or she needs help. If there is no response, move in to contact the victim. Reach across your body and grab underneath the victim's opposite upper arm with your fingers out and back and the thumb

in and forward, palm up. Kick to get moving, and pull the victim's upper arm back across your body as you roll the victim from a face-down to a face-up position. Once the victim is turned, level and move into an appropriate tow (see Figure 4.25).

Front passive wrist contact. This contact is similar to the upper arm contact, with the exception that you grab the wrist instead of the upper arm. Approach the passive victim from the front, reach across, and grab the opposite wrist, palm down. As you begin kicking to get started, pull and turn the victim on his or her back. Depending on the size of the victim, it might be easier to exaggerate the turning motion by making a large *U* motion as you pull to turn the victim.

Front active swim around contact. Executing a rescue of an active victim carries a greater degree of danger to the rescuer and to the victim. To reduce the risks of active victim rescues, it is recommended that you approach the victim from the rear to maintain an element of control of the situation. Therefore, when approaching an active victim from the front, swim around to the rear before contact is made. If the victim follows you around in a circle, keep talking to him or her and reevaluate the situation. If the victim is

4.24 Rear active cross-chest contact

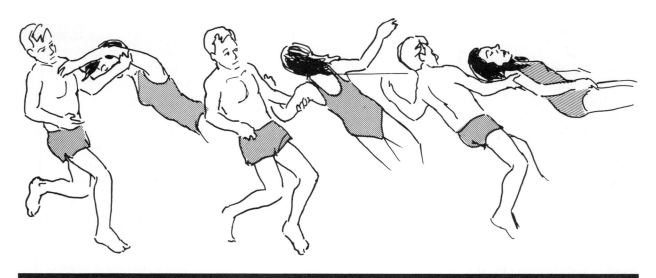

4.25   Front passive upper arm contact

strong enough to swim around, he or she may not be in immediate danger, and you might be able to calm him or her down. On the other hand, if the victim is extremely active, he or she will tire and give you a chance to get to him or her safely. If the victim does not respond when you ask if help is needed, swim around to him or her quickly, staying a safe distance of approximately 2 ft beyond his or her grasp. If the victim remains facing the shore, continue swimming around to his or her back side and execute a rear active contact, described on page 46. After the victim is placed in a control tow position, level off and support him or her. Encourage the victim to relax.

Contacting a submerged victim.   With a submerged victim, time is critical. To locate the victim, look for surface bubbles in the water, especially if the water is not clear enough to see through. Bubbles will continue to be squeezed from the victim's lungs the deeper he or she goes. Before you dive under to look for the victim, make sure you have released your rescue equipment. When you surface again, you can use it for rescue purposes. Once you've located the victim, grab the hair, an armpit, or wrist. If the victim is heavy, use a bear hug or armpit grip from the rear and push off the bottom. On soft bottoms avoid pushing off or you might find your-

self knee deep in mud. Depending on the circumstances, tow the victim to safety or begin artifical respiration (mouth-to-mouth resuscitation). Getting oxygen to the victim is a priority in this situation. If a spine injury is suspected, take special precautions. The procedures for a spinal injury rescue are discussed in chapter 5. Keep in mind that initial contact of an unseen submerged victim is a frightening experience. Be prepared for it and act accordingly.

Tow

After you have contacted and leveled the victim safely, you will have to move into a position to tow the victim to safety. Maintaining control of the victim, keeping his or her face above the surface, and his or her body close to horizontal will help you minimize resistance and proceed to safety quickly. Keep the following in mind when deciding which is the best tow to use to get the victim to safety:

- Distance to be towed
- Weather and water conditions (cold, waves, calm water)
- Size of the victim
- Your own level of fitness or skill
- Condition of the victim (active or passive)

Armpit tow. The rear armpit tow is the most versatile tow for an unconscious victim and maintains the movement initiated by the rear armpit contact. With a passive victim, grab under the armpit, right arm to right arm or left arm to left arm. The hand should grip with the fingers inside and the thumb outside. The towing arm should be as straight as possible, thus maintaining some distance between the victim and rescuer.

Hair tow. For a long-distance tow and an unconscious victim, a hair tow might be the most effective. Level the victim off; then slide the palm of your hand from the base of the head toward the forehead, fingers spread as they run through the hair. As your hand reaches the forehead, grab as much hair as possible. Keep your arm straight and wrist cocked to avoid letting the victim's face submerge (see Figure 4.26). If the victim has long hair, then your fingers should be bent so the fingernails and palm run along the hair to the front of the head. This helps prevent the fingers from getting caught in the victim's hair.

4.26   Hair tow

Head tow. After the initial contact is made with the victim, position your hands so that the middle finger is over the jaw and the palms cover the ears, as shown in Figure 4.27. Using the inverted breaststroke kick, swim directly behind the victim to safety. Keep your arms straight and the victim's face above the water.

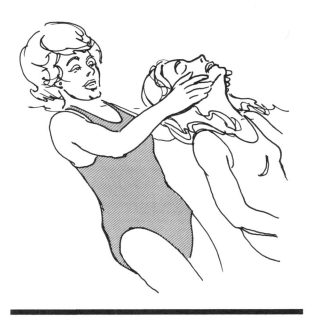

4.27   Head tow

Cross-chest tow. Utilize the cross-chest tow on conscious calm victims. The cross-chest tow is a continuation of the cross-chest contact, discussed on page 46. Maintain the position as you swim to safety. Be careful to support the victim's lower back with your hip and avoid putting pressure on the victim's neck and throat.

Control tow. Should a conscious victim become panicked and suddenly begin struggling, you can move from a cross-chest to a control tow. This tow should only be used until you can calm the victim and begin an arm stroke again. Without losing contact of the cross-chest position, make a fist with the arm that is flat against the victim's chest; then grab your wrist with your free hand over the top (thumb to the inside and your fingers to the outside) until you have a secure grip under the victim's armpit. The fist and wrist grip (control) would all take place behind the victim's armpit, as shown in Figure 4.28. This would pre-

4.28   Control tow

vent the victim from attempting to separate the rescuer's hands in a panic situation because the rescuer would be behind the victim. In the case of smaller rescuers, he or she must secure the wrist as close to the back of the armpit as possible, then continue kicking to safety. This tow will slow your progress.

Don't be afraid to submerge (keeping the victim at the surface) and continue kicking. Surface to breathe and roll with the struggling victim. Encourage the victim to relax. If the victim does become calm, you can resume a normal cross-chest tow.

Surf tow.   Used predominantly at the beaches (hence, "surf" tow), the surf tow, illustrated in Figure 4.29, is a variation of the cross-chest that

4.29   Surf tow

is recommended for short distances only (5-10 ft). After the initial contact, slide your arm under the victim's arm and across the victim's chest. For additional support, slide both arms around the victim and grab the wrist that is already across the chest.

Collar tow.   If the unconscious or passive victim is wearing a shirt, grab the collar of the shirt, palm down, and tow to safety, maintaining a straight arm (see Figure 4.30). Swim directly behind the victim and encourage him or her to keep the head back.

Tandem tow.   In a case where the passive victim is very big, you may want two people to contact and make a rescue. The most effective use of the tandem tow is when both rescuers use the armpit tow from positions on either side of the

4.30 Collar tow

victim. The victim may be towed in either a front- or back-floating position, depending on the water conditions.

Two-person tow. In a double-drowning situation or in any situation where two people are locked together, you can tow both victims for a short distance. Preferably, use either armpit or collar tow. If the victims break apart, you can do any of the following:

- Tow the weaker victim to safety and return for the second victim.
- Position both on their backs and using the armpit tow, tow both.
- Support one with a flotation device.

The situation and condition of the victims will play a large part in your decision-making steps.

Double Drowning

In a double drowning, a *lifesaver* has failed to get free of the panicked victim, and both have gone under. You, the *lifeguard*, must make some quick decisions: primarily whether you should tow both victims to safety together; or whether you should separate them, tow one, then come back for the other. First, bring both to the sur-

face. If you decide to separate the victims, approach the original victim from behind (this victim will be the one with a tight grasp around the head or neck of the other). Submerge both; grab under the armpits of the first victim. Place your foot on the shoulder of the "would-be rescuer" and push. As they separate, move to a control tow and take the victim to safety as quickly as possible, returning then for the would-be rescuer. If you decide to tow both together, use the two-person towing techniques discussed previously to enable you to move as quickly as possible.

Defenses and Releases

The possibility always exists that a seemingly passive victim can without warning become panicked and grab for you. Though this reaction is unexpected, you can plan ahead for a reaction. As you assess the situation and determine the best course of action, always anticipate the possibility of something going wrong and plan a defense or release for every contact that you choose. In a split second, you may not have time to consider the options. In addition, between the time of your initial identification of the emergency, the assessment of the situation, and the time it takes you to reach the victim, the condition of the victim could have changed drastically, making it important for you to not only maintain eye contact but also to have several options open for the rescue.

The technique of the defenses and releases are the same. The difference is the point at which the victim has a secure grasp on you. Practice the techniques at different stages. If you cannot get control of the situation for lack of air, panic, or weakness, use the release to escape, regain your composure, and reevaluate the situation before proceeding with the rescue. When you are practicing these skills with a partner, be sure to determine a release signal (i.e., a pinch or warning tap) ahead of time to avoid possible injury to a "pretend" victim.

Defense

A defense can be defined as a movement that enables you to *avoid* being grabbed by a panicking victim. If you somehow lose control of the situation, your first priority is to regain control. The ability to maintain control directly affects your own safety and your ability to effect a rescue. Use an effective defense that will give you a few moments to reevaluate the options and to regain composure and control of the situation. In the traditional definition of defense, you maneuver to avoid being grasped. As a professional lifeguard, you may not need the time to get away and then come back to regain control. If this is the case, use the defense as a step similar to a release to move into a control tow. The main point is to emphasize the importance of assessing the situation and being prepared to react and adapt to changing circumstances to regain control of the situation.

Suck in, tuck in, duck in.   In any rescue situation, it is imperative for you to maintain control of the situation. As a trained guard, you are prepared for any emergency; but even if you are prepared, most emergencies don't follow along with the rule book, and the bottom line is that you are in a life-threatening situation. Knowledge, experience, and trained reactions are on your side.

For a lifeguard caught off guard, the following three things should be instinctive.

1.   In a situation where the victim becomes the attacker, (a) *suck in* air (take a quick breath), (b) *tuck in* your chin and turn your head to the side to keep the victim from grabbing your neck, and (c) *duck in*, using your hands to force yourself under the surface (see Figure 4.31).
2.   Get oriented: Assess your situation, and get set to act.
3.   Act in an explosive manner to get away.

It is very difficult to simulate a life-threatening situation. While you may hope that you never have to experience this situation, the possibility could become a reality. If you ever have to exercise Steps 1 and 2 above, unless you exercise Step 3 successfully and get away, you could yourself become the victim of a double drowning. That is the purpose of the watermanship drills on pages 87-88: These drills simulate a life-threatening environment as closely as we are able to reproduce it.

4.31   Suck in, tuck in, duck in

One-hand block.   As you approach the victim from the front and before you start to swim around to the rear, a current or wave may push you closer to the victim than you anticipate. If the victim grabs for you, block with a straight arm with your elbow locked. Your palm should hit the victim in the upper middle part of the chest. As you block, duck under the water to avoid the victim's grasp. This is critical for lifeguards with shorter arms. The safe and ideal contact point is the upper chest; however, if the hand strays a bit to the throat or face, the technique is still effective.

If the victim has grabbed your arm as you do a one-arm block, depending on the size of the victim and the distance to be towed, keep your arm straight; encourage the victim to relax and to hold on to your arm, and keep kicking to shore. This is called the *block and tow*. However, if the victim tries to climb your arm and is unable to listen to you, then use a release method described on pages 60-61 to escape the grasp.

Block and turn.   The block and turn is not a defense by pure definition; however, the principle involved is based on defensive tactics. As you approach from the front and the victim grabs for you, use a one-hand block with a straight arm to the chest. Immediately grab the victim's upper arm (fingers out, thumb in), slightly below the elbow with your free arm. Duck your head under as you push the arm over your head, turning the victim around as shown in Figure 4.32. You could opt to push and kick to get away at this point or to maintain body contact with the "block" arm throughout the turn. Release your "turn" arm (maintaining body contact), and reach over the victim's shoulder to his or her armpit. Grab your wrist to complete the cross chest control tow. Encourage the victim to relax and proceed to shore.

Two-hand block.   If the victim attempts to grab you from the front around the head, stretch both of your arms out and place them against the victim's upper chest. Push hard, then kick to get away (see Figure 4.33).

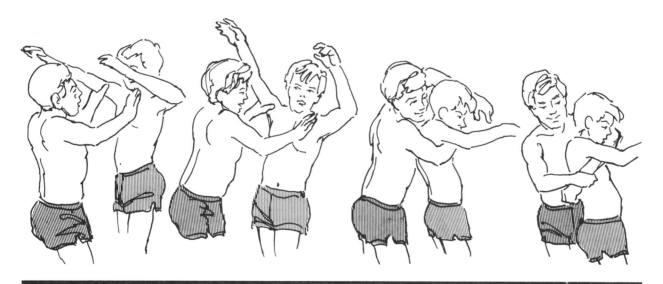

4.32 Block and turn

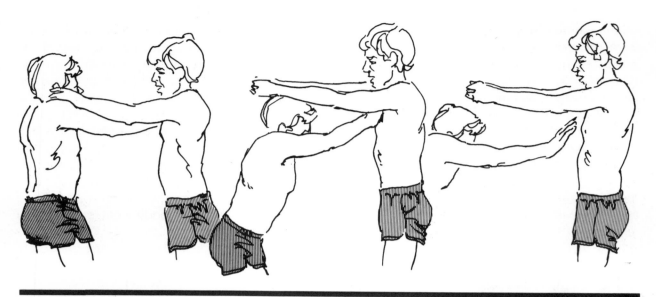

4.33   Two-hand block

Foot block.   Approaching from the front, as the victim grabs for you, reverse your position with one leg bent at the surface (toes are on the surface of the water) with foot flexed. Push the sole of the foot against the victim's chest and straighten your leg. If the victim grabs your leg, you can either use your other foot on the victim's shoulder to push away or to submerge him or her when you straighten your leg. The foot block can be used after any defensive move where control is not taken. It is much better to have someone grab for your leg than for your head or neck.

Rear pivot breakaway.   If you are caught by surprise and a victim tries to grab you from behind, you must react quickly to avoid a tight grasp around your neck. Take a quick breath, tuck your

head in, and turn the head to the side. Duck your head underwater and pivot halfway around, using your elbows to clear the way. As soon as you are facing the victim, put your hands on the victim's hips and push with the heel of your hand. As you push the hips, you could opt to get away by pushing off and kicking away from the victim; or you can turn the victim, pushing with one arm and pulling with the other, and maintain body contact with the push arm. Slide the pull arm up and do an armpit lift. Follow with the other arm, reaching over to a cross-chest control tow (see Figure 4.34).

Front parry.   The front parry would probably be used in an ocean or a wave pool where the victim would be moving toward you from a high position, such as from the crest of a wave. As the

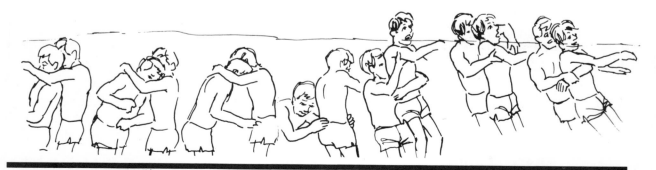

4.34   Rear pivot breakaway

victim comes toward you, grab under his or her right arm just above the elbow and push him or her aside with your right arm as shown in Figure 4.35. You can also parry with the left arm. Use the victim's momentum to your advantage. You can then move to an appropriate contact and tow.

Front head defense. When you are caught off guard from the front and the victim is about to grab your head, remember to first take a quick breath (suck in), tuck your chin, and turn your head to the side (tuck in). As the victim lunges for you, submerge (duck in), reach up, grab

underneath the upper arms (thumbs in, fingers out), and push up forcefully (see Figure 4.36). At this point you can escape and get away to reevaluate the situation, or you could complete the move. Hold on to the victim's arms. Turn the victim halfway around by pulling one arm and pushing the other. Maintain chest contact with the "push" arm. Then immediately reach the "pull" arm over the victim's shoulder across the chest and around to the armpit. Grab your wrist with your other hand to complete the cross-chest control tow. Encourage the victim to relax and proceed to shore.

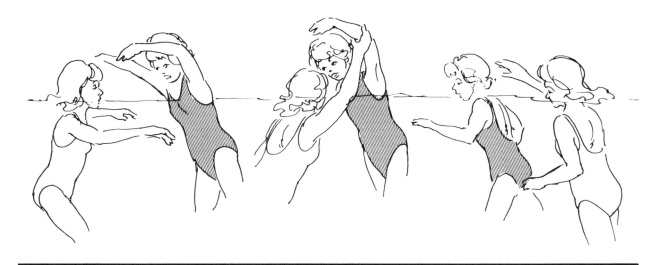

4.35 Front parry

4.36 Front head defense

Releases

When you rescue an active victim, there are any number of reasons to assume the victim will do something unexpected. For that reason, it is imperative that a lifeguard be proficient at releases. The main difference between a defense and a release is that a release is a move to escape the grasp of the victim, and a defense is a move to avoid the victim's grasp. If a defense doesn't work for some reason, then the guard most likely will have to use a release. In a situation where you are grabbed from behind, it will probably be totally unexpected because you would never knowingly turn your back on a panicked victim. It is possible that a submerged victim could surface behind you and grab you from the rear. In this situation, it is imperative that you act quickly. *Suck in, tuck in*, and *duck in*, immediately to protect your neck. Use an appropriate release and regain control of the situation. Depending on the accident situation, you may choose to get completely free of the victim, reevaluate the situation, then regain control of the situation.

Front head hold—Hip push away.   If the victim grabs you in a front head hold, take a quick breath, tuck your chin in and turn your head to the side. Place the palms of your hands on the victim's hips (fingers out), and push the hips away with the heels of the hands. This will give you

the chance to slip out of the victim's grasp. Turn the victim 180°, maintaining body contact. With your other hand, grab the victim's upper arm as you kick to the surface. Complete the release by reaching over the victim's shoulder with your push hand to secure a cross-chest control tow (see Figure 4.37).

Front head hold push-up.   If the victim grabs you from the front, take a quick breath, tuck your chin, and duck your head to the side. As you submerge, the victim may release the grasp and try to get to the surface. Give the victim a moment to see if this might be the case. If not, bring both your hands up and grab the victim's arms from the bottom (thumbs in, fingers out). Push up forcefully, freeing yourself from the victim's grasp. Proceed with the technique used in the front head defense discussed on page 55. Turn the victim, and move into a cross-chest control tow.

Front head hold with body scissors.   If you are in a tired swimmer's assist, and for some reason, the swimmer becomes panicky, he or she might try to grab your head with his or her arms and your body with his or her legs. Remain calm and keep swimming as long as you can still see and breathe. If, however, the victim pushes your face underwater, you must react. Place both of your hands on the victim's forehead, keep kicking, and push the victim's head back so his or her nose and mouth are underwater. Normally, the victim will release his or her arms because of the

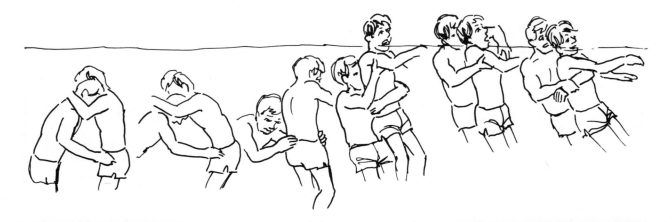

4.37   Front head hold—hip push away

water in the nose and mouth. Be careful not to push the victim's head and neck so far that you risk possible injury to the neck. If the victim does not release the legs, continue pushing him or her down. When the victim releases his or her legs, normally he or she will flip to the stomach (see Figure 4.38). Swim out of the victim's grasp, and lift him or her, using an appropriate armpit, chin, or head lift to the surface. Place the victim in a cross-chest control tow. Be careful when you practice this in a class setting. Your pretend victims are trying to hold on tight to simulate a panicked victim, and you could hurt them easily by pushing their head back too far.

Bypass. If the victim has you in a front head hold, keep swimming and if suddenly they collapse most likely because their head is pushed under water, cutting off their air, reach down and grab the victim's back or shoulder to keep him or her from sinking. With the other hand, reach inside close to your face and place your hand on the victim's other arm. Push his or her arm down and move around to his or her back, maintaining contact with the arm that is supporting his or her back, as shown in Figure 4.39. Move into a cross-chest tow. Once the victim gets air, he or she may regain consciousness.

4.38 Front head hold with body scissors

4.39 Bypass

Rear head hold—Rear pivot. If the victim grabs your head from the rear, take a quick breath (suck in), tuck your chin and turn your head (tuck in), and submerge (duck in). The victim may release you naturally and will try to return to the surface. If not, continue turning the direction you ducked your head, using your elbows to clear the way. If the victim has gotten a secure grip on your neck during the initial head hold, turn your body from the neck down to avoid possible injury to the neck. Once you are facing the victim, push the hips away while you turn the victim halfway around. To turn the victim, one arm will push as the other arm pulls. Maintain contact with the arm that pushed, and use the pull arm to do an armpit lift. Then move to an immediate control tow and proceed to safety. This move is similar to the rear pivot breakaway on page 54. The difference in the moves is the point at which the victim actually gets a grip on you.

Rear head hold—Pullover. If the victim grabs you tightly behind the neck, take a quick breath (suck), tuck your chin and turn your head (tuck) as you submerge (duck). Give the victim 3 to 5 seconds to release you naturally. If he or she

doesn't release you, reach up and grab the victim behind the head (using both hands, over the ears), or grab as much hair as possible. Roll forward, pulling the victim over your head. Keep kicking to avoid slowing the pullover action. As the victim releases, move to a control tow (as shown in Figure 4.40).

Rear head hold with body scissors. If the victim grabs you from the rear with his or her arms and legs, take a quick breath (suck in), tuck your chin down and to the side (tuck in) push yourself under the surface (duck in), and flex at the waist as you submerge to keep the victim from getting a stronger hold on you (see Figure 4.41). Then use one of the following elbow releases to get free of his or her legs before proceeding with an appropriate rear head hold release.

Single elbow release. To escape from the victim's locked legs using the single elbow release, grab the victim's top foot securely, placing your palm on the top of the foot with the thumb around the ball of the foot, and place your elbow on the victim's top leg between the calf muscle and shin just below the knee area. Grab the bottom of the foot with the other hand. Pull the foot toward your abdomen while you push

4.40 Rear head hold—pullover

out with the elbow until the victim releases the leg lock as illustrated in Figure 4.42. Once the legs are released, continue with head hold release. If this move is done correctly, the victim's arms and legs will release, allowing you to get out of his or her grasp and move into a control tow.

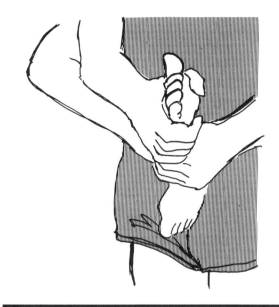

4.42 Single elbow release

4.41 Rear head hold with body scissors

4.43 Double elbow release

Double elbow release. Depending on the position of the victim's legs around you, you might want to use the double elbow release. Repeat the steps above with the exception that you will use both elbows placed inside each of the victim's legs between the calf muscle and the shin bone to push outward (see Figure 4.43). Regardless of the method you choose, in a life-threatening situation brute force might be needed to effect the proper escape. As the legs release, continue with the appropriate head hold release and move to a control tow.

Double grip on one arm. If the victim grabs your wrist with both hands, immediately make a fist with that hand (thumb side up, little finger down) to prevent a possible injury during the release. Then grab your fist with the other hand. Pull both arms back quickly toward your shoulder, bending the elbows to give the pull more leverage, as illustrated in Figure 4.44. If necessary, use a foot block on the victim's chest to get clear of the grasp.

Double grip on one arm—Draw under. If the victim grabs your arm, start swimming as in the block and tow move. If the victim begins to panic and starts to climb your arm, first grab his or her arm or wrist with your hand, if you can, locking wrists to keep the victim from climbing farther up your arm. Then draw the victim under and turn yourself 180° around to a side-by-side position. Reach your near arm around his or her shoulder and head and grab his or her inside arm. Lean forward so he or she cannot breathe momentarily, until the victim lets go. Release your locked wrist and draw him or her up. Immediately move into a control tow as pictured in Figure 4.45.

Front over and under. If the victim grabs you from the front with one arm over your shoulder and one arm under your other shoulder, place the free arm (upper arm) across his or her face and the other arm under his or her upper arm. Push the victim's face outward as you push his or her upper arm up and turn him or her around. Maintain chest contact with the hand that was on the victim's face. As he or she turns, move to a control tow as pictured in Figure 4.46.

Rear over and under. If the victim grabs you from the rear with one arm over your shoulder and the other arm under your other arm, first tuck your chin to the side and down. Place your lower hand underneath the victim's upper arm, and push up as you slip under the victim's arm and away, as shown in Figure 4.47. Keep your other arm straight as you slip under and out of their grasp. Continue to turn the victim, and move into a control tow.

In any emergency, the panicking, drowning victim has probably not read this book and will grab anything in any way that he or she can to avoid drowning. While there is a fine line between a release and a defense and while professional lifeguards and aquatics professionals will probably debate the line for years to come, in an emergency, the point is not whether you used

4.44 Double grip on one arm

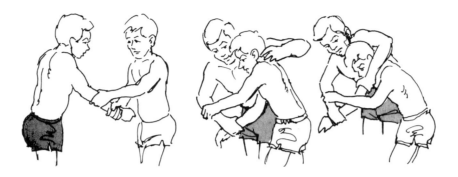

4.45   Double grip on one arm—draw under

4.46   Front over and under

4.47   Rear over and under

a defense technique or a release technique; it is, however, whether you were confident enough with the techniques to modify them to fit the appropriate situation and save a life. That demands practice, patience, and performance.

Carries and Water Exits

Once you have towed the victim to safety, you have to get him or her out of the water as quickly as possible to start the emergency treatment necessary considering the nature and severity of the accident. Conditions such as geographical location, terrain, size, and strength of the rescuer as well as assistance available from the side or shore play a role in determining the type of exit you elect to use.

Carries

One-person drag. This is probably one of the quickest and most efficient ways to get an unconscious person from a lake or ocean. From behind the victim, encircle your arms under the victim's armpits and grab your own wrist to lock your grip. Walk backward dragging the victim's feet. Be careful to lift with your arms and legs and not your back. If you are having difficulty maintaining a tight grip on the victim, you may find it easier to grasp the victim's opposite wrists to secure your grip, as shown in Figure 4.48.

Two-person carry. If you are the second rescuer at the scene and join in the carry just described, you should face the first rescuer and pick up the victim's feet with one leg at each side of your body. Move to safety in this position.

Pack back carry (butterfly turn). As you reach waist-deep water, release the tow, grab the victim's right wrist with your right hand, and grab the victim's left wrist with your left hand (palms down, thumbs back, fingers forward). Push the victim's right arm under and between you and him or her, turning in and spinning 180° so that the victim's chest is on your back. Hold the victim's arms to your chest and walk up and onto the beach as illustrated in Figure 4.49. Be sure you are carrying the victim on your back and not supporting his or her weight by his or her shoulders.

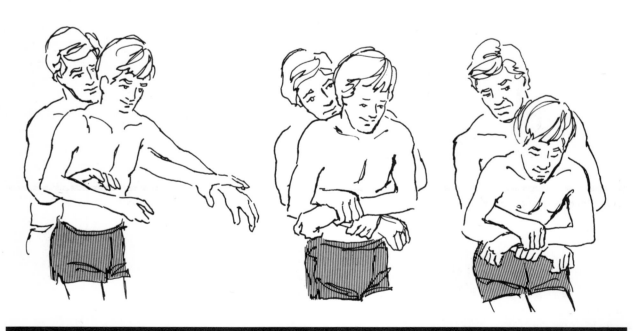

4.48 One-person drag

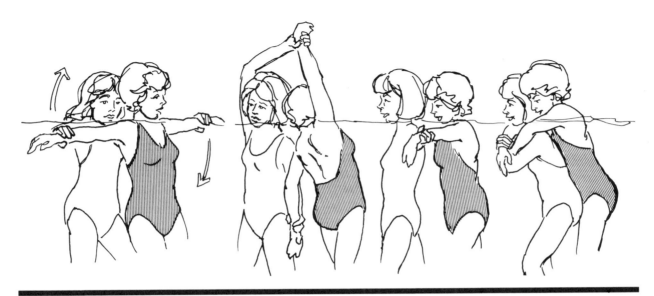

4.49 Pack back carry (butterfly turn)

Piggy-back or straddle back carry. Depending on the height of the victim, move from a pack-back carry by holding both of the victim's wrists in one hand, reach and hook the victim's legs (at the knee) around your arm with your free hand, change hands and repeat (see Figure 4.50). Move to safety.

Saddleback carry. In rough or beach terrain, the saddleback carry distributes the victim's weight, allowing you to move more easily. Move the victim to a back-floating position in waist-deep water. Place the victim's far arm across the back of your shoulders. Slide your near arm under the victim's far arm immediately below the armpit and across the back to support the head. Bend your knees and lower your back as you turn 180° to back into the victim. Try to get the victim's stomach in contact with your lower back. With the victim's arms over your shoulders, reach back behind and under the victim's knees, hooking them over your arms. Hold the arms for support. Lean forward as you rise to distribute the weight more evenly (see Figure 4.51). In deeper water it may be necessary to use the left hand to hold the face out of the water, but as soon as the victim's weight is felt and the head is safe, move the left hand back to the shoulder-back position to avoid the possiblilty of causing a neck injury.

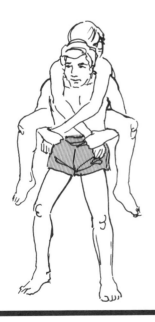

4.50 Straddle back carry

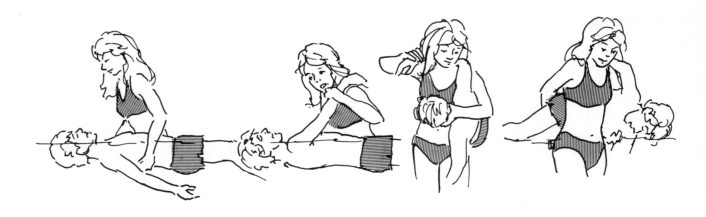

4.51   Saddleback carry

Let down.   When you carry a victim to safety, remember to lower him or her carefully to the ground to reduce the chance of additional injury. On land or a solid surface, step forward and kneel slowly and lower the victim's legs gently. Maintain contact with the victim as you turn around and lower the victim to a lying position, supporting the head, as shown in Figure 4.52.

Supporting assist.   If the victim is conscious, but very weak, assist him or her to safety. Stand in a side-by-side position, pull his or her near arm across your shoulder, and secure it with your far

hand. Your free arm should support the victim's waist. Walk to safety.

Multiple person carry.   Depending on the area and the facilities available, the situation may warrant a multiple person carry. This carry takes coordination of the rescuers involved and should be practiced in shallow water or on the deck if mats are available. The rescuer located at the head of the victim should coordinate the lift commands. For a three-person carry, two rescuers are on one side and the other is facing them on the other side. All three rescuers kneel close to the

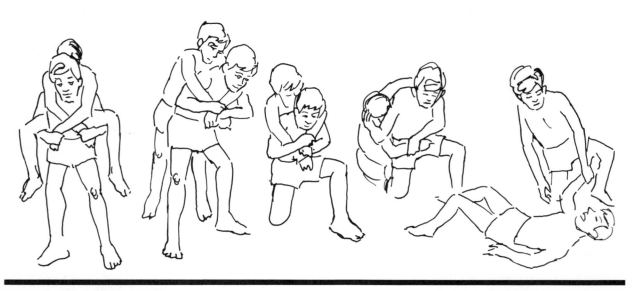

4.52   Let down from a straddle back carry

victim: Rescuer 1, at the head, supports the victim's head and back; Rescuer 2, on the opposite side of the victim, supports the back and hips; Rescuer 3, next to Rescuer 1, supports the victim's hips and legs. With their grips secure, Rescuer 1 gives the signal, and all three rescuers synchronize their movements and proceed to safety. If the carry is used on dry land, Rescuer 1 gives the signal, "ready" and "lift," and all three lift the victim to their knees. There they secure their grip. Rescuer 2 locks arms with the other two; Rescuer 1 then gives the command, "ready" and "stand." When you are ready to lower the victim, Rescuer 1 reverses the lift action. Figure 4.53 illustrates the procedure.

Deep Water Exits

In deep water once you have towed the unconscious victim to the side, support the victim while placing his or her hands on the deck or pier one hand at a time. If the distance between the deck level and the water level is too great, call for additional help. To remove the victim from the water, maintain a secure support of the victim's hands as you move to the side and slide out of the water.

Straight arm lift.   Grab the victim's wrists and lower the victim before lifting to gain leverage and make the lift easier. Keep in mind that the victim's head may be leaning forward. As you lift, take care to lift the victim straight to protect his or her head from possible injury. Likewise, be careful to use the appropriate lifting technique to avoid possible injury to yourself. As the victim's hips clear the deck level, step back and lower the victim slowly, turning his or her shoul-

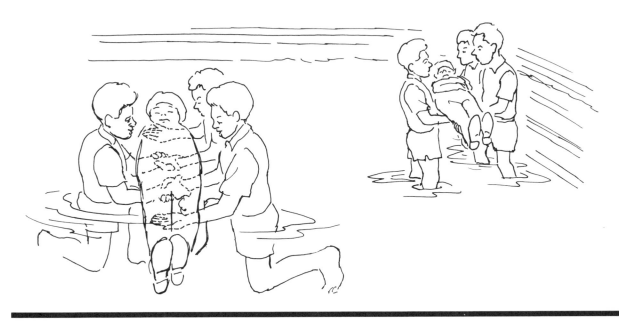

4.53 Multiple person carry

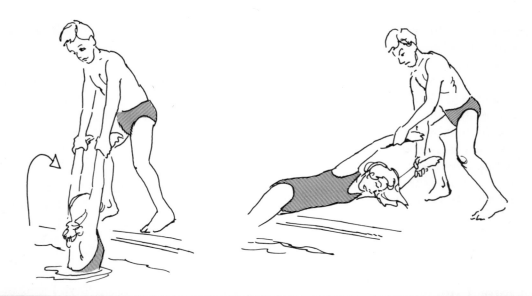

4.54   Straight arm lift

ders to the side so that one arm can be placed under the head before it hits the pool deck or dock. This acts as a pillow and prevents head injury. Let go of the arms and grab the legs and slide them onto the deck surface (see Figure 4.54). Roll the victim to the back and be prepared to begin emergency procedures.

Cross-arm lift.   If the victim is small, you may want to cross your arms, and, as you lift, turn the victim to a sitting position on the deck (see Figure 4.55) and lower them carefully to a lying posi-

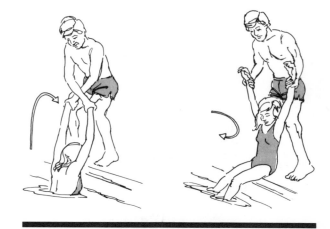

4.55   Cross-arm lift

tion. Place your foot on the deck where his or her head will rest; this will act as a pillow.

Once you have moved the victim out of the water, your responsibility is still not over. Assess the condition of the victim and begin first aid. Follow the emergency procedures set up for your facility in regard to certain emergencies. Fill out the pertinent reports and notify the appropriate people. Use courtesy and diplomacy in dealing with the final details of an emergency.

Review Questions

1. What is the first step in making an effective rescue?
2. List five guidelines for early detection of potentially weak swimmers before entering the water.
3. List five guidelines for early detection once the swimmer is in the water.
4. List and explain the use of two pieces of rescue equipment that would be appropriate in (a) a pool environment, (b) an open-water environment, and (c) a surf environment.
5. Why is it important to maintain eye contact with the victim once you have determined that a rescue is necessary?
6. (a) Explain the quick reverse maneuver and (b) its basic purpose.
7. After contacting a victim, what is the purpose of leveling him or her off before towing?
8. List five factors that help determine what tow will be the most appropriate to use in a certain situation.
9. Explain the difference between a defense and a release.
10. In an emergency situation when you have been caught off guard, list and explain three steps that are crucial for you to instinctively execute a successful escape.
11. In any rescue situation, what is your first priority?

chapter 5

SPECIAL RESCUES

A professional lifeguard always faces the possibility of an unforseeable situation taking place that warrants special attention. Although these situations occur infrequently, their consequences are potentially severe. The following are guidelines to help identify these situations and to take quick action.

Spinal Injuries

The primary principle in handling a spinal injury rescue is to keep the head and neck in their normal and natural positions with relationship to the rest of the body. Any suspected head or spinal injury should be treated as such until proven otherwise. Take special care not to aggravate the injury. Determining whether a spinal injury situation exists is difficult. Obviously, witnessing the accident is your best clue. The location of the accident could also indicate signs of a spinal injury. Is it around a diving board? Is blood detected on the board? Is it in shallow water? Is blood in the water or coming from the victim's mouth or nose? If you detect any of these signs, do not take any chances. Treat the accident as a spinal injury.

In a spinal injury situation, the circumstances are, for the most part, less than ideal and further complicate rescue. A mishandled spinal injury could result in permanant damage, if not death. If the victim is face down in the water, you must turn him or her over as soon as possible to establish breathing; however, the rest of the rescue should be done at a slow, deliberate pace. As a professional, you must be proficient at this type of rescue.

Approach the victim with a suspected spinal injury cautiously, being careful not to make unnecessary water movements. If the victim is face down, you will have to turn him or her to face up. This is the first critical step in the recovery. The vise grip technique, illustrated in Figure 5.1, has proven to be suitable in various situations and effective for different skill levels.

Approach the victim carefully from the side. Place your arm along the length of the midsternum (breastbone) region. At the same time, place your other arm along the upper thoracic area of the victim's spine. Your hands should not touch the victim's head until your arms are in place. With the arms in place, cup one hand under the back of the victim's head. Be careful not to touch the victim's neck or cervical area. Your other hand firmly supports the victim's chin

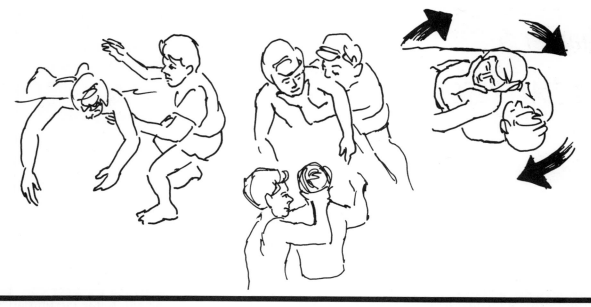

5.1   Vise grip

along the jaw bone. Lock your wrists and press your forearms together, creating a "vise" that immobilizes the victim's body. Hold this position during and after you have turned the victim.

To turn the victim to a face-up position, you will have to submerge slowly (being careful not to lose your grip), slide under the victim, and come up on the other side. This should bring the victim to a face-up position. Remember, speed and accuracy are critical in this type of rescue.

An advantage of this technique is that rescue breathing may be started without changing positions. Monitor the breathing process carefully and make sure the airway stays open as you proceed to safety. If artifical respiration is necessary, use a modified jaw-thrust technique to open the airway. Do not tilt the head back, for this could cause additional damage.

Once the victim is stable, secure him or her to a spine board before removing the victim from the water (see Figure 5.2). Position the straps on the board, turn the board sideways, and push it underwater. Float the board up under the victim for even contact. Packing sand bags along the sides of the body and head before securing the straps will increase stability. You can use surgical collars to aid immobilization but do not rely upon them to provide more than 30% to 40%

5.2   Securing a victim on the spine board

of the support. Do not use any packing under the head or neck. The head should be secured solely by a strap across the forehead.

To remove the victim from the water, place the board perpendicular to the poolside, dock, or water's edge in shallow water. Once you have secured the victim on the board, the person at the head gives the lift commands (see Figure 5.3). Lift the board vertically upward, being careful not to tilt or rotate it as you pass the board to rescuers

5.3 Removing the victim from the water on a spine board

on dry land. On dry land, follow through with emergency procedures until transfer to the appropriate facilities is available. Practice this technique with the guard staff at your facility. Coordination and team work will save time and will maximize the effectiveness of the rescue.

Deep Water Rescue Breathing

In open water, when you come upon a victim who is submerged or face down in the water and is not breathing, you will have to tow him or her for a distance. To increase the chance of survival for that victim, getting air into his or her lungs is critical. In this type of rescue, equipment will be extremely useful in either increasing your buoyancy or that of the victim. This added buoyancy will give you better leverage to do rescue breathing in deep water (see Figure 5.4). Without equipment, you must exert great effort to tread water and maintain the position. This technique will take much practice.

After you have recovered and leveled a submerged or face-down victim who is not breathing by using a chin pull with one hand, use your free hand to turn the victim's head; then pull the corner of the mouth down, and let any water run out. Then take the free arm and hook it over the

victim's near arm and under the back, as shown in Figure 5.5, cradling the neck between your thumb and forefinger. Release the chin-pull hand, and press with the heel of the hand on the victim's forehead, tilting the head back to open the airway. Pinch the nose closed with your thumb and forefinger (see Figure 5.6). Turn the head toward you, and seal your mouth over the victim's. Continue this process while kicking at a slight angle, toward the victim's feet. The

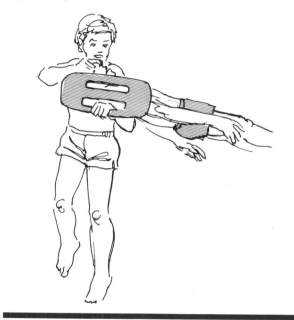

5.4 Breathing using equipment

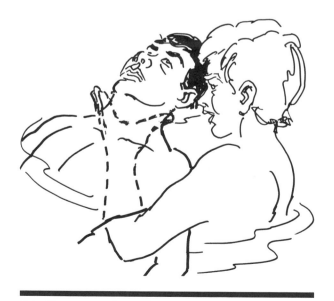

5.5 Deep water breathing step 1

5.6 Deep water breathing step 2

momentum should help keep both of your faces out of the water.

You should be able to feel the air pressure building up in the victim's lungs. If not, tilt the head back farther and try again. If the victim has water in the lungs, it may be difficult to get air in. Blow gently at first to avoid pushing the air into the stomach. Blowing too hard and forcing air into the stomach could cause the victim to vomit. The vomitus will not hurt you; the smell, taste, and look makes it unpleasant to experience. If vomiting should occur, clear the mouth first by sweeping the vomitus out with your finger so you do not blow it into the lungs. Once you reach safety, remove the victim from the water and continue rescue procedure until emergency personnel arrive to take over.

Scuba-Diving Safety

The growing sport of skin and SCUBA (self-contained underwater breathing apparatus) diving and the increased involvement of the YMCAs across the country in training their members to participate in this sport places a new emphasis on the need for lifeguarding skills related to scuba diving. It is necessary to expand your lifeguarding thinking to include rescue procedures that are suitable for the type of equipment and clothing used by the scuba diver.

Scuba and skin divers should be in special areas, separated from the other swimmers. Their equipment could cause a severe injury should a collision between a diver and recreational swimmer occur. In an open-water setting, make sure that the diving area is marked off with a flag attached to a buoy as shown in Figure 5.7. During instructional scuba- or skin-diving classes, swimmers should be restricted from the diving area.

The YMCA and other national organizations have certification standards for scuba divers. Facility administrators will set a policy to determine which "C" (certification) cards will be accepted for admission to their facility. It should be strongly stressed that only divers with current "C" cards should be admitted to use the facility.

If you suspect that a scuba diver is missing, take the following steps immediately:

1. Determine from others where the diver was last seen.
2. Move to that area and look for bubbles.
3. Put a search group of at least two divers into the water immediately to search the area. Use a predetermined search pattern (see pp. 76-77).

5.7 Diving flag

4. If the time interval is lengthy, send for help, such as the lake patrol, emergency personnel, the sheriff, or others.
5. Determine the possibility of the person leaving the diving area without notifying the group.

Be aware of possible currents that could alter the missing diver's location. Where currents are present, conduct the search, working in a downstream direction. In some circumstances, a diver might encounter difficulty underwater that would cause him or her to panic even if he or she got to the surface. If a diver is struggling on the surface, proceed in the following manner:

1. Move toward the victim while giving verbal encouragement.
2. Extend a floatable object (if available) to the victim.
3. If it is necessary to make a swimming rescue, approach from the rear and (a) grasp the victim's tank at the neck and press up on the opposite side to bring the victim to a level position, (b) remove the victim's weight belt, (c) inflate the victim's buoyancy compensator (BC) and tow him or her to safety. Always stay below and behind the victim, and (d) be sure to watch the victim at all times.

If the victim is not struggling, then he or she is probably unconscious and needs immediate resuscitation. If this is the case, take the following steps:

1. Reach the victim in the shortest amount of time possible.
2. Turn the victim face up.
3. Remove the victim's weight belt and other heavy objects. However, leave the tank on but vent it to let the air escape, making the tank buoyant.
4. Inflate the BC on the victim if he or she is wearing one.
5. Proceed with mouth-to-mouth resuscitation immediately.
6. Move the victim to shore as resuscitation continues.
7. Move the victim immediately to a doctor or a hospital.

8. Engage any assistance available, and provide direction to those able to help.

Scuba diving emergencies require special attention. Air embolism and decompression sickness accidents both require immediate recompression, so time is of the essence. In areas where scuba diving is permitted, the lifeguard must know the location of the nearest recompression chamber and the procedures for providing transportation of the victim to the facility. Specific rescue procedures may vary depending on the area you are guarding; however, the basics for determining those procedures can be developed through CARE—cognizance, assessment, rescue, and evacuation.

Cognizance

The signs exhibited by a potential scuba victim are often quite subtle. The exhausted scuba diver on the surface may suddenly and quietly slip beneath the surface for no apparent reason. It is possible that the potential victim's ego may stand in the way of his or her ability to express anxiety, illness, or other distress to his or her diving partners or to others. Scuba equipment often conceals facial expression and other gestures that signal stress or anxiety, which sharply curtails the possibility of verbal communication. Often, signs of distress are not easily recognizable; however, the following behaviors can be considered indicators of trouble to the alert lifeguard:

- High treading or finning with sufficient vigor to lift a major portion of the body and equipment out of the water
- Rejecting mask and/or regulator mouthpiece
- Clinging and clambering—pulling the body toward the high point of any object on the surface.
- Diving alone
- Lack of motion—apparent unconsciousness
- Giving distress signals—raise one arm, whistle, and so on.

Assessment

In assessing the severity of the problem, consider the following issues:

- Nature of the problem (e.g., the environment, physical distress, equipment problems, anxiety)
- Status of the victim
- Training and physical conditioning of the potential rescuers
- Available assistance in the form of equipment or other personnel

Rescue

The chief advantage in rescuing a scuba diver is that you can use the diver's equipment to establish positive buoyancy, to assist in breathing, and generally to stabilize the victim while still in deep, open water. However, the diver's equipment can be dangerously disadvantageous if it is unfamiliar to you.

When establishing contact with a victim of a scuba diving accident, there are certain priorities that should determine your actions. Although the priorities are essentially the same whether the victim is at the surface or submerged, the manner in which you react may differ.

If the victim is on the surface, establish buoyancy by removing the weight belt. Communicate with the victim. If the victim is conscious, reassure and encourage him or her to help wherever possible, for example, in establishing buoyancy.

If the victim is underwater, make contact with and stabilize the victim before you move him or her. Then surface to the side or behind the victim. Remove the victim's tank if you anticipate a tow over a long distance or through kelp, weeds, surf, or rocks. Once you have stabilized the victim, try to get help.

You will rarely be called upon to rescue a submerged diver. However, if ever in such a case, immediately release the diver's weight belt. This will cause the diver to break free of the bottom and begin to float toward the surface. If the diver does not break free, establish positive buoyancy by manually using the auto inflator by blowing into the BC. The CO_2 has an all-or-none release valve and may easily cause an ascent that is too rapid; therefore, use it only as a last resort.

Because the diver has been breathing compressed air, it is important for you to force the air from the victim's lungs during the ascent. From behind the victim, bring your hands around the victim's chest and continuously apply force upward and toward your body during the ascent. If you do not follow this procedure, the air in the victim's lungs will expand as the water pressure decreases during the ascent. This expansion may cause an air embolism or a rupture of the alveoli, or air sacs, in the lungs.

During the ascent to the surface, keep the victim's head level. To ensure this, use a chin-pull hold on the victim, keeping one hand free to activate the auto inflator. The victim will become more buoyant as you ascend. If you have the time and the opportunity, purge some air out of the BC during ascent. If, prior to and during the ascent, you have not inflated the victim's BC, inflate it at the surface, either by pulling the proper cord or by blowing into the inflation tube. You also may want to take off the victim's tank at this time if you haven't already done so.

Towing the victim may be difficult due to the nature of the equipment design. You may use a tow similar to the "shirt" or "collar" tow by grasping the victim's tank valve or BC straps rather than the collar.

Evacuation

In a situation where you rescue a scuba diver, after-care of this victim will vary from the care given to a nondiver victim in one important aspect. When a diver is in trouble, an air embolism is always a possiblity. The victim should therefore be transported in the Tendelenburg (feet raised/head lowered) position. This position should be maintained when the victim is being lifted onto a boat, into a vehicle, and then being transported to a medical facility. Obviously, other first-aid procedures should follow as necessary.

Victims of a scuba accident may need a special facility for treatment. Be aware of the nearest decompression chamber or how to locate it. *DAN*, or the Diving Accident Network, is located at the Duke University Medical Center in

Durham, North Carolina. This agency is open 24 hours to answer questions regarding diving accidents and can be reached by calling 919-684-8111.

Search Procedures for Missing Swimmers

Time is critical when you are searching for a submerged victim. The use of mask, fins, and snorkel will greatly enhance your rescue effort by providing a greater area of clear visibility. However, in some open-water swimming areas, the visibility is limited. The following procedure will help you facilitate the rescue of a submerged victim in an open-water area.

1. If a swimmer is suspected to be missing, alert staff immediately.
2. Encourage the person who reported the missing swimmer to remain calm and give a complete description of the missing swimmer and the location where last seen.
3. Make an announcement specifying the name, description, last location of the missing swimmer, and where additional information about the swimmer should be reported.
4. During the announcement, instruct designated lifeguards to check the water area, bathrooms, showers, locker rooms, snack bars, and other adjacent areas.
5. Depending on the personnel available, have someone call the swimmer's home or check their living quarters (if vacationing).
6. If the person is still missing, guards must concentrate on the water area. Clear the swimming area and begin search procedures.

Guards can also organize volunteers to aid in the search of the shallow water. If the swimmer is not found after a thorough search, call in additional professional rescue squad personnel.

General Principles

In shallow water with poor visibility, instruct volunteers or guards to link arms or hold hands and wade in a line across the area. The line should progress forward slowly, rescuers making careful sweeping motions with their feet. Care should be taken not to disturb too much of the bottom. A guard should coordinate each group, and volunteers should not go beyond chest-deep water.

In deeper water, standardized search patterns are suggested for specific circumstances. No search can be completed in an orderly manner without planning and preparation; however, these standard patterns should simplify the organization of a recovery effort. If a search is prolonged, the chances of a rescue are diminished; the search then becomes a recovery rather than a rescue. Plan ahead to save valuable time. A planning board pulled by a boat increases the speed of a search, but care must be used to prevent injury to lifeguards or swimmers.

Deep Water Search Method

In searching, adjust the extent of each sweep of the pattern to the visibility in order not to skip over an area. Also, keep in mind that the victim may not be lying on the bottom. In a line, guards should surface dive down to the bottom, and complete a predetermined number of strokes before surfacing. They should use a sweeping motion with their arms during the stroke, just above the bottom to avoid stirring up the sediment. To cover low-visibility areas completely, stay close enough together to slightly overlap another diver's sweep. In deep water, guards should complete a designated number of strokes, surface almost straight up, and move back about 6 ft before reforming their line and diving down again (see Figure 5.8). A guide line formed with one guard on the surface will allow directional control because when the guards come to the surface, they will be able to see the guide. Where visibility is better, extend a line between divers to maintain spacing. With clearer water, divers can rely on sight instead of touch and consequently can swim closer to the surface to expand their field of vision and the area covered. A set of hand signals to indicate recovery or the need to surface should be established so that all divers will understand and comply.

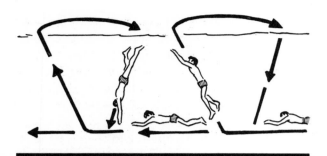

5.8   Standard search technique

Search Patterns

In deep water, lifeguards should work together in one of the following search patterns to find the missing swimmer:

• Circular pattern search
• Grid pattern search
• Parallel pattern search
• Diagonal pattern search

Circular pattern for flat lake bottom.   From a fixed center point, search a circular area. Space the distance from the center dependent upon water clarity. Expand the circle with each revolution, and make certain that a marker is placed at the starting point to assure complete coverage of that circle (see Figure 5.9). The distance out from the center is readily controlled by a line attached to the final center point and is held by the diver. In murky water, the free hand (hand

not used to hold the line) may be used to search by touch. Guards should try not to disturb sediment while searching. The rope attached to the center post should be kept taut on each sweep at the distance desired for searching. The anchor line of the boat can be used for the center of the circle, or a weight may be placed on the bottom, providing it is heavy enough to remain fixed.

Grid pattern for irregular lake bottom.   Tie ropes to divide the area to be searched into small units so that the area can be covered thoroughly (see Figure 5.10). Guards may search one unit

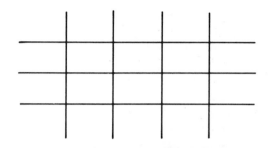

5.10   Grid pattern search technique

and then move to another, saving time from being disoriented. The ends of the ropes should be weighted, with float lines projected to surface for marking purposes. If necessary, one edge may be lifted and relayed to form a new area. Leave one edge anchored to eliminate possibility of an area not being covered. The size of the units is optional, but the units should not be more than twice the visibility in width. Two or more divers can be assigned units to search before moving to another unit.

Parallel pattern for irregular shoreline.   The guide or controller should walk along the shore holding a line extended to a diver who is searching the visibility range from the shore. By keeping the line taut and at right angles to the shoreline, the area may be thoroughly searched. Space each search pass to the limit of visibility, and complete the search.

Diagonal pattern for river currents.   Swim at right angles to the shore because the current nat-

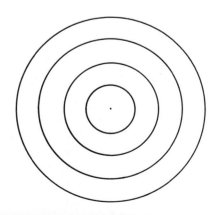

5.9   Circular pattern search technique

urally carries you on an angle. This will eliminate the necessity to fight water movement if you attempt to swim directly across from the starting point. After crossing the current, return in the same manner (see Figure 5.11). Second and successive searches may be started downstream from first starting point and parallel to it. It is important to search quickly because the victim may drift with the current.

3. Extend yourself as far as you can on the unbroken ice while keeping your lower body as close to horizontal as possible.
4. Work your way onto the ice. If the ice breaks again, keep using this method until you reach stronger ice. Once you are out, stay low and distribute your weight over as much surface area of the ice as possible as you move to get off the ice (see Figure 5.12).

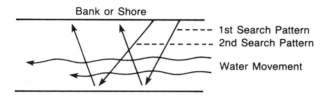

5.11 Diagonal pattern search technique

Ice Rescue

Although activities in the water are not as enjoyable as the seasons change and as the temperatures cool, winter activities on the water draw large numbers of enthusiasts outdoors to enjoy ice skating, hockey, or fishing, especially in the northern United States. These activities can be fun and safe as long as you know about the area you are using and about the conditions that will make that area safe. Generally, small areas such as ponds, small lakes, and slow-moving streams are the safest. The ice should be frozen to at least 4 in. in depth before being used. Newly formed ice is not as strong as older ice; however, in the spring, the older ice is subject to spring thaw and begins to lose its consistent thickness. Keep in mind the season of the year during which you skate or move onto the ice. It is important in determining the safety of the ice conditions.

If you or someone with you breaks through the ice, follow these guidelines:

1. Stay calm; don't try to climb out immediately.
2. Kick behind you to avoid being pulled under the ice.

5.12 **Stay low and distribute your weight over a large area to move off the ice**

If you try to help someone who has fallen through the ice, be careful not to fall through yourself. Stay low and try to find something, for example, a ladder, branch, rope, or board to reach to the victim. If no equipment is available, grab the victim's wrist as shown in Figure 5.13.

5.13 **Ice rescue**

Encourage the victim to stay calm and kick to get into a horizontal position as previously described. Once you have pulled the victim to safety, get him or her to a shelter and administer first aid immediately. Treat for hypothermia.

Submerged Vehicle

As a professional lifeguard, the chances of you ever having a submerged vehicle in your area are slight; however, the fact that 60% of drownings happen to people who never intended to go in the water warrants your knowledge of this information. If you ever face a situation of this nature, make sure before you act to have someone around you call for a rescue squad immediately.

Generally a vehicle that enters the water from a height of approximately 6 ft or less and lands on its wheels will float for varying amounts of time; however, once a vehicle begins to submerge, it will sink in less than a minute. The vehicles float longer with the windows up, giving more time for escape or rescue. Once underwater, they sink at a steep angle, possibly coming to rest on the roof in water 15 or more ft deep. Unless they sustained damage on impact, windows can be opened at any point during the descent of the vehicle; however, in the absence of structural damage, doors cannot be opened until the pressure inside the vehicle is equal to the pressure outside. In front-engine vehicles, an air pocket forms and will be forced into the rear and possibly to the trunk area until the vehicle come to a rest. At that time, the air moves back into the passenger section. Normally, because of the small size of the air pocket, the ability to open doors and windows is not affected.

Studies (e.g., Kuhn, 1961) have shown that people wearing safety belts have a greater chance of surviving the initial impact with water. If the vehicle is floating in the water, wheels down, the best technique to escape is through an open window before the water rises to the window level. If the vehicle sinks too quickly to escape, stay

in the rear to take advantage of the air pocket and plan an escape either by opening the nearest window or door, as soon as the pressure has equalized, or pushing out the rear window. Remember, power windows will not operate once the power has been cut off and will need to be broken. Because of the composition of the window (tempered glass), it can be broken by a hammer and should shatter when pierced. Water will gush in through an open window after the vehicle begins to submerge. The force of the water may make it difficult to get through the window at that time.

If you attempt to rescue a person in a submerged vehicle, be aware of the possibility of entanglement from bent car parts that could hook on your clothing. If a vehicle has submerged with all the windows up, the best way to get to the passengers may be by breaking the back window. If you are trying to get a passenger out as the vehicle submerges, be careful of the force exerted by water entering through the window.

First Aid for Special Situations

In order for your facility to be better aware of the needs of its patrons, encourage people with special health considerations to keep a confidential file on record with the administrative staff for reference in case of an emergency. For special situations, act in compliance with your aquatic agency. If applicable, notify parent or responsible adult that first aid was needed and notify appropriate medical personnel.

Epilepsy

Often the person involved knows when a seizure is coming on and may have his or her own medication on hand. An attack can be brought on by nervous tensions, resulting in involuntary contractions of the muscles in the legs, arms, or body. According to the Epilepsy Foundation of America, in the case of an epileptic seizure in the water, you should take care to prevent the victim from injuring him- or herself during the seizure. Support the victim, preferably away from the poolside, and keep his or her head above the water. When the seizure has passed, assist the victim out of the water and stay with him or her until medical assistance arrives.

Under these circumstances, it will be difficult for the victim to help in his or her own rescue. In addition, it will be hard to determine whether the victim's condition (after you remove the victim from the water) is due to the effects of the seizure or to a near drowning. It is important to call for medical assistance for any seizure victim, for complications could arise as much as an hour after the apparent recovery.

Heat Exhaustion

Heat exhaustion most commonly occurs when people have not become acclimated to exercising in extreme heat. The body temperature rises and the cooling mechanism cannot keep up with the rising temperature. This causes an imbalance in the system. The symptoms are cold, clammy, sweaty, and pale skin, accompanied by faintness, dizziness, or nausea. To treat heat exhaustion, have the victim lie down, raise the feet 8 to 12 in. and loosen the clothing. Administer small sips of salt water (1 tsp/8-oz glass) every 15 min. Apply cool wet cloths to the skin and fan the victim or move him or her to a cooler room.

Heatstroke

Heatstroke is more dangerous than heat exhaustion. In heatstroke, the sweating mechanism is blocked and the body cannot cool itself down; therefore, the skin is hot, red, and dry. Immediate first aid is necessary to reduce the body temperature. Monitor the victim closely. Undress or loosen the victim's clothes. Then sponge the victim with cool water, apply ice packs, or place him or her in a tub of cool water. When the temperature goes down, dry off the victim. If the temperature starts to rise, begin the cooling process again. Do not give stimulants. Get the victim to the hospital as quickly as possible.

Heart Attack

A heart attack usually results from a clot or blockage in one of the vessels that supplies blood to the heart. It has been called a *coronary, coro-*

nary artery thrombosis, coronary occlusion, or a *myocardial infarction.* Basically, all mean that there is a blockage of blood flow to the heart muscle, the myocardium. The victim of a heart attack could lose consciousness and die immediately or may just show signs of shortness of breath, chest pains radiating from the neck down the left arm, and gray or bluish skin color. If the victim is conscious and has medication, administer that medication. Keep the victim calm and comfortable and seek medical assistance immediately. If the victim is not breathing, begin artificial respiration.

Because drowning and heart attack are causes of sudden death, a lifeguard should be trained in CPR. Heart attack is the number one killer in the United States, with more than 684,000 deaths annually: that is, 54% of all deaths. Some deaths occur in water. For many years, it was thought that in the event of drowning the only necessary steps were to drain the water from the lungs and to initiate some form of rescue breathing. Current research, however, has found that if breathing is ceased due to suffocation (by water), then the heart muscle will cease pumping shortly because it has not received enough oxygen. Certain conditions following the ingestion of water during drowning create an imbalance in electrolytes (which differ between salt and fresh water) and an increased blood volume, which will also cause heart stoppage.

Though some victims may never show any warning signs, some may have an uncomfortable feeling of a squeezing pressure in the chest, indigestion, or swelling in the ankles. If these symptoms last longer than 1 or 2 minutes, the victim should be encouraged to consult medical treatment. Be aware that some victims may be vehement in their denial of the seriousness of the symptoms.

If someone shows signs of a heart attack, keep him or her comfortable, preferably sitting, depending on the victim. Then call for help. This includes the rescue squad, the doctor, and sometimes the hospital. When calling a squad, be sure to do the following:

- Give your name, location, and phone number.
- Tell them the victim's symptoms and what you have done.
- Wait until they tell you to hang up to be sure that they have all the information they need.

Never transport a patient yourself. Always use an ambulance! If someone has a cardiac arrest while you are on duty, activate the EMS (emergency medical service) system in your facility, and proceed with CPR until medical personnel arrive. Remember these 10 steps:

1. Determine the victim's consciousness.
2. Call for help.
3. Position the victim to begin CPR.
4. Open the airway.
5. Check for breathing.
6. Ventilate the lungs.
7. Clear obstruction from mouth, if necessary.
8. Check pulse and breathing.
9. Activate EMS.
10. Begin CPR.

Fractures

The two types of bone fractures are closed and open. A *closed*, or *simple* fracture, is not associated with an open wound. An *open*, or *compound* fracture, accompanies an open wound and is much more serious than a closed fracture, primarily because of the risk of infection. The signs of a fracture are swelling, tenderness to the touch, deformity, and sometimes pain on motion. Provide first aid as follows:

1. Do not move the broken limb.
2. Keep the victim quiet.
3. Control hemorrhaging, if any, with sterile dressings.
4. Treat for shock.
5. Do not move the victim unless he or she is in immediate danger.

Signs and treatment for dislocations are similar to those for fractures: Keep the injured area quiet and obtain medical attention. However, the key is to immobilize the injury. Do not attempt to reposition a dislocation or a jammed injury.

Shock

Shock is a condition that results from the depression of vital body functions. Shock can become life threatening even if the trauma that caused it is not. In the instance of shock, the blood in the body moves into extravascular tissue, thus reducing the volume of oxygen-carrying blood in the system. The result is a decrease in oxygen reaching the brain, and the person may become unconscious. Left untreated, it could become life threatening.

In the early stages of shock, breathing is shallow and irregular, the pulse is rapid and often too faint to feel in the wrist, and the skin may be pale. The inside of the lips or eyelids will be blue. In the late stages of shock, the eyes become vacant and lack luster, the pupils become widely dilated, and the skin becomes blotchy and mottled. The victim could lose consciousness.

The goal of treatment for shock is to improve the circulation, increase the supply of oxygen, and maintain the normal body temperature.

1. Keep the victim lying down. If there are no head injuries or heart problems, his or her feet may be elevated slightly (8 to 12 in.); but if you are in doubt, leave the victim flat.
2. If the victim is lying on the ground or floor, place a blanket beneath him or her. Cover the victim only sparingly, according to the temperature of the environment. (Do not cause the victim to sweat—it is better to keep him or her slightly cool.) If there is no injury to the head or chest, you may slightly elevate the victim's legs (8 to 12 in.); but when in doubt, leave the victim flat.
3. Call for medical help immediately.

Head Injury

Head injuries should be suspected in any accident due to force. The victim of such an accident should be immobilized because a fractured skull or broken neck may or may not be present.

The signs and symptoms of a head injury may be any or all of the following:

1. Pupils of the eyes are unequal in size.
2. Bleeding from the nose, ear canal, or mouth.
3. Clear or pink fluid draining from the nose or ears.
4. Possible paralysis of one or more extremities.
5. Face may be pale, flushed, or normal.
6. Pulse may be slow and full, fast and weak, or normal.
7. Headache is usual and sometimes associated with dizziness.
8. Vomiting.
9. Blurry vision.
10. Sleepiness.
11. Difficulty in awakening.

If the victim is unconscious, and you do not suspect possible back or neck injury, place a small pillow or its equivalent under the head. Loosen clothing about the neck, and if the victim is awake, have him or her lie flat. Whether the victim is conscious or not, do not administer liquids. If a dressing is needed for a scalp wound, merely lay a large sterile dressing over the injury and then apply a bandage. Get medical help immediately.

Simple Cuts, Scrapes, Wounds

Around an aquatic setting, minor cuts and scrapes are a daily occurrence and can usually be handled easily by cleaning the affected area thoroughly and applying a sterile bandage. Be careful to use a soap that is anti-allergenic to avoid any adverse reaction to the cleansing. Depending on the severity of the accident, you may want to suggest that the injured person see a doctor.

In the event of a more severe wound, apply direct pressure to the wound with a sterile dressing and elevate. If a sterile dressing is not available, use your hand. If the direct pressure method does not stop the bleeding, apply pressure to the artery supplying blood to the wound. The two most important pressure points are the brachial and the femoral. The *brachial* is located on the medial side of the humerus (inside of the arm) between the biceps and the triceps. By pressing

it against the bone, the arterial flow will be reduced enough to allow for better clotting. If the victim is bleeding in the leg, compress the *femoral* artery. This artery is located near the groin where the leg attaches to the body. Apply pressure to this artery with the heel of your hand.

Hypothermia

The hypothermia victim will be shivering violently with possible muscular rigidity. To treat a mild case of hypothermia in which the body temperature is no less than 95°, begin by removing the victim from the cold environment and into a building or shelter that is protected from cold air. Remove all wet clothing and have the victim take a warm shower or a warm bath if facilities are available. If facilities are not available, sitting by a warm fire or placing heating pads on the heat loss areas may be helpful. Such treatment is safe because of the relatively small change in body temperature. Get the victim into warm clothing. Drinking hot coffee, tea, or cocoa is good to help warm the victim. However, do not give alcoholic beverages: They act to reduce the shivering mechanism which creates the heat that will bring the internal core temperature up to normal. Where shivering in the water lowers the survival time, shivering on land in a warm environment is beneficial. Shivering is the body's own safety mechanism to create more heat because the core temperature is below normal. The muscles can create 3 to 5 times the heat when shivering as compared to resting.

Depending on the situation, in an outdoor environment, keep the victim calm and close to a fire. You may have to share your body heat with the victim to speed rewarming. As the core temperature rises, the victim may experience what is known as *after drop*. This is due to the fact the the cold blood from the extremities mixes with warmer core temperature blood and the result is a drop in body temperature. Keep the victim as still as possible to minimize the effects of after drop.

When the victim has been in the water for a period of time and the core temperature is 94° or below, get the victim to the hospital. Wrap the victim in a blanket to begin the rewarming process and apply heating pads to the heat loss areas. If the victim is weak and can hardly stand, warm the victim as quickly as possible. The most effective way is a warm bath. The victim's arms and legs should remain out of the water to prevent after drop. The water temperature should start at a tepid 82°, and over a 10 to 15 min-period the temperature should be increased up to 104° to 106°. Putting the victim in the warmer water too soon would be quite painful and could cause burns or tissue damage.

The victim of immersion hypothermia with a body temperature of 94° and below will have white or pale gray skin with some cyanosis. Signs that the victim has warmed enough are a clearing mind, skin color flushing to red or pink, and the victim feeling better. At all times during the rewarming process, monitor the victim's respirations and pulse.

If the victim is semiconscious or unconscious, administer no fluids of any kind. In addition, watch for possible vomiting. If vomiting does occur, clear the victim's throat immediately with your fingers; this clearing will prevent aspiration of any vomitus into the lungs.

If the victim can walk, then the lifeguard may attempt the rewarming process. However, if the victim's temperature falls below 90° and if foggy thinking is evident along with weakness and the inability to walk, wrap the victim in a blanket to prevent further heat loss. Keep movement of the victim to a minimum to reduce after drop, and arrange immediate transportation to an emergency care facility. Rewarming of these severely hypothermic victims should be done under the supervision of a physician. Only in a remote environment should a lifeguard attempt the full rewarming process.

Review Questions

1. If you suspect a victim to have sustained a spinal injury, list the steps to get that person to safety.
2. List three steps that you must execute in order to perform deep-water breathing successfully.
3. What does SCUBA stand for?
4. If you suspect a diver is missing, what should you do?
5. Explain the rescue of a scuba diver by using CARE.
6. Briefly explain a search-and-recovery pattern for (a) a flat lake bottom, (b) an irregular lake bottom, (c) an irregular shoreline, and (d) a river current.
7. If a victim has an epileptic seizure in the water, what is your primary action until the seizure is over?
8. Explain the difference between heat stroke and heat exhaustion.
9. (a) What are the warning signs of a heart attack? (b) What steps should be taken if you are faced with a heart-attack situation?
10. (a) List the signs of a head injury; (b) list the procedures to treat a head injury.

chapter 6

LIFEGUARD RESPONSIBILITIES

In addition to the skills you must develop to be a good lifeguard, you must also accept responsibility for your actions. As a professional lifeguard, you are a part of a highly trained team, and your actions reflect on your whole agency, including those who work with you. Swimmers who come to your facility will notice your behavior whether you are on duty or off. Likewise, your respect for the rules and procedures, and for your own physical condition and appearance will reflect on your agency as a whole.

Keep in mind that your primary goal as a lifeguard is to protect the safety of all swimmers in your area: first, by preventing accidents, and second, by responding to an emergency quickly and efficiently to minimize the danger of everyone involved. This goal is accomplished by (a) having the lifesaving skills to do your job and being in good enough physical condition to use these skills, and (b) knowing the information specific to the type of aquatic area you are guarding and communicating it responsibly and diplomatically to your patrons.

In addition, once you have accepted the responsibility of taking the job as a lifeguard, you have also accepted the legal and moral consequences of your actions and decisions. When you accept the responsibility of protecting the public safety, you are accountable for your knowledge and actions.

The guidelines for your specific duties, communication, public relations, organized group swimming systems, and physical conditioning will be covered in this chapter. The job of a lifeguard is not static and no two situations may ever be the same. Therefore, this information presents basic guidelines for consideration as you develop specific procedures to meet the needs of your facility.

Duties

As a professional lifeguard, you must make the following duties become habit:

1. Report ready for duty, at least 15 min before your assigned shift; be in proper uniform and position when you go on duty.
2. Have the proper protective equipment for your station: a rescue can or another piece of equipment, sun helmet, sun glasses, whistle, towel, sunscreen lotion.
3. Be professional, alert, courteous, and always tactful.
4. Be alert to observe signals from other guards.
5. Know the proper emergency procedure for your area in case of an accident.
6. Avoid unnecessary talking or visiting with swimmers. If talking is necessary, do so while keeping your assigned area under observation.
7. Maintain observation of your area at all times.
8. Enforce all facility rules.

9. Use a courteous but determined manner to correct rule infractions. If the problem persists, report it at once to the head guard or manager.
10. Try to explain the reason you are enforcing the rule and the danger involved.
11. Keep swimmers and bathers from congregating on walk areas in the immediate vicinity of the guard stands.
12. Refer detailed inquiries to the head guard or manager.
13. Not only guard the lives of the patrons, but also maintain discipline among the more active people to ensure the comfort and pleasure of others. Do not tolerate any rowdiness.
14. Clear all swimmers from the water during an electrical storm.
15. Keep swimming area clean and fit for inspection at all times.
16. Keep all litter picked up.
17. Check to be certain all doors and gates to the swimming area are locked when a lifeguard is not on duty.
18. At closing time and between each change of activity make a survey of the bottom of the swimming and wading areas.
19. If employed at a beach or open body of water, be familiar with bottom conditions: also have knowledge and the required skills to make a rescue using small-craft equipment.
20. Keep all lifeguard, lifesaving, and first-aid equipment in good repair and ready, and know how to use it.

Communication

Effective communication is probably the single most important element in determining your efficiency as a lifeguard. Communicating with people and other guards is of vital importance. Without communication, very little can be done to control or to prevent accidents in, on, or around the water.

Whether verbal or nonverbal, the three main objectives of communications that you must consider are:

1. to explain and enforce safety rules and regulations in all swimming areas;
2. to keep people from getting into dangerous or potentially dangerous situations, areas, or currents;
3. to provide direction to all persons to provide control within your area in case of emergency or accident; and
4. to notify other waterfront supervisors or authorities of emergencies and to summon such assistance as might be needed.

All communications must be simple, clear, direct, and easily understood.

Sometimes nonverbal communication such as a gesture, a look on your face, or a nod can be as effective as a comment. The key to good communication is making sure that the content of the message you are sending and the emotion you are using to send it are appropriate to the situation and to the age group.

However, good communication is inconsequential if you cannot be seen or heard. Your uniform and whistle are primary tools for effective communication, automatically establishing you as the person in charge. Always report to work neatly and properly attired because your uniform—your shirt, shorts, bathing suit, hat, and whistle—immediately identifies you in a crowded area.

In addition to communicating effectively with the swimmers in your area, you must be able to communicate with the other guards. Follow a procedure set up to handle the needs of your facility. If none has been established, develop one. The signals you use (e.g., one short whistle blast to get a guard's attention, two short blasts to get a swimmer's attention, one long blast to clear the pool, and three short blasts to resume activity) are not as important as the consistency of using them. Once your facility has an emergency signal system in place, use it, and educate swimmers to the system. Some facilities ask guards to clear the pool twice a day; this helps to educate swimmers as to what the signal means as well as gives the guards a chance to break and survey the pool area. Other areas clear the pool every hour to allow for a 10-min adult swim. The signal procedure must meet the needs of the particular aquatic environment. Whatever the procedure, consistency is the key to its organizational effectiveness. Review the system at weekly staff meetings to reinforce the consistency.

In addition to signal communication, a cover system must be developed at any facility to ensure the protection of all swimmers at all times. During an emergency, if one guard must leave his or her position, another must be available to cover both positions. The guard may have to move to a better vantage point to be able to adequately cover the new area. The exact way in which an emergency coverage is set up will depend on the location and distance between stations and on the number of personnel available. It is important, however, that the cover system result in minimal confusion.

Remember, every area having swimmers must be guarded at all times. When emergency coverage goes into operation, each waterfront supervisor not active in the rescue will be responsible for a larger area. Emergency coverage begins when a guard signals an emergency and will follow the system developed as needed.

When two guards are present at a facility, one of them should stay on the stand to guard the whole area and to control the crowd, which may require moving to a more advantageous position. That guard will enter the water only if absolutely necessary. A swimming facility with more than one guard on duty should be divided into overlapping zones to leave relatively small areas that are not watched by two or more guards. The facility having a larger patrol with a number of lifeguards should have an extensive emergency cover system.

Public Relations

Public relations may be viewed from several perspectives. The most obvious is how the general public interprets what it sees and hears from you. Public relations may also be viewed as the way you interact with your peers, staff, superiors, or subordinates. Because your behavior is always scrutinized, you can help provide an excellent climate in which good public relations can develop by following these guidelines:

- Always maintain a well-groomed personal appearance.
- Avoid gossiping, laughing, joking, and reading while on duty.
- Be courteous to patrons at all times. Avoid shouting or arguing.
- Direct any questions that you cannot answer to a superior.
- Never report to duty or or be on duty under the influence of alcohol or drugs. This will result in immediate dismissal.
- Never abuse the authority you are given. This reflects not only on you, but on your whole organization.
- Cooperate with your fellow guards. Work as a team.
- Be thoroughly familiar with your area and its potential hazards.
- Always refer the media to the appropriate organizational spokesperson regarding any accidents or drownings.

In conclusion, just good, plain, ordinary common sense and courtesy will go a long way in accomplishing your mission and will make your duty pleasant, satisfying, and rewarding.

Organized Group Swimming Systems

Most camps and youth organizations use one or more safety check systems to account for each individual quickly. These systems allow the lifeguards and staff to be aware of the number of children in the water and their location. This becomes especially important in a lake or river where the bottom is not visible.

Buddy Systems

In the buddy system, each swimmer is paired off with another swimmer of equal ability. These pairs of swimmers are called buddies. Buddies must stay close to each other at all times. At a certain signal, such as two short whistle blasts, all partners immediately join hands and raise them in the air, remaining stationary as they do so. Those in charge can then easily count the number of pairs. In the case of an uneven number of swimmers, one pair of buddies should be a threesome. When all swimmers are accounted for, the leader repeats the original signal, allowing the swimmers to resume their activities. Make sure that the signals used for "buddy up" and "all clear" are different from any other signals used by the lifeguard staff.

Roll Call or the Tag Board

The roll call and tag board systems function similarly. Roll call is taken *before* and *after* each swim period. If an individual does not respond, a search is immediately begun. For the tag board system, a board with hooks may be erected at the waterfront. Everyone is given a tag with his or her name written on both sides to hang on the board. Color coding the sides makes it easier to identify who is in or out of the area. Before the swimmers enter the water, they turn their tags to the "in" side; upon leaving the water, they flip their tags to the "out" side. Then at the end of each period, the leader can easily check to see if all swimmers have left the water by looking to see if any tags are still turned to the "in" side. If a tag is unaccounted for, an immediate search must be started. It is imperative that the leader enforce the rule that each individual *must* respond to his or her own name at the roll call and that each individual *must* be responsible for turning his or her own tag. Their safety depends on it.

Cap System

In the cap system various colors of bathing caps are designated for each swimming level. The following is a widely used system:

- Nonswimmers and beginners wear red.
- Intermediate swimmers wear yellow.
- Advanced swimmers wear blue or green.
- Leaders and lifeguards wear white.

A guard can easily spot a red or yellow cap that is in an advanced swimmers' only area and can take immediate action to bring that person to a safer place. The cap system may be used in conjunction with any of the other systems.

In all organized swimming, it is important for the instructors and lifeguards to make a quick check of all persons in their care. Any method that works should be employed to ensure their swimmers' safety.

Physical Conditioning

In any physical activity, it is very difficult to maintain your skills without practice. In lifeguarding, if you are doing a good job, you are trying to prevent having to use your lifeguarding skills by preventing accidents from happening; yet at the same time you must be ready to respond to an accident as a professional. This paradoxical situation led Charles E. Silvia (1965) of Springfield College, Springfield, Massachusetts to develop the concept of watermanship drills. While daily lap swimming is important to fitness, these drills were designed to give lifeguards a chance to practice their skills in a somewhat competitive setting. In addition, lifeguards (or lifesavers) develop endurance, breath control, agility, skill, and emotional fitness in and under the water. Simulating a life-threatening situation and its accompanying pressure is difficult; however, these drills will help you develop confidence, quickness, and insights of lifeguarding.

Watermanship Drills

First, make sure you have adequate space to practice and that the water is deep enough the avoid hitting the bottom. Use *spotters* (other guards) to keep each other from hitting the sides of the pool. Start out with basic skills like kicking across the pool, face down or up with your arms above your head. Then proceed to kicking and doing a front somersault and resume kicking across the pool. You can add variation to this drill by pushing off the side, doing a half-front somersault, ending on your back and kicking back to the side. Keep your arms extended to protect your head.

Once you have mastered basic somersaulting and twisting in the water from a glide position, continue the moves for different variations:

1. Long, shallow dive; glide; kick; full twist; kick; front somersault; and kick to the side.
2. Long, shallow dive; glide; kick; ½ turn to your back; kick; back somersault; glide; and kick to the side.

Contact Drills

As you become more confident in the water, proceed to the contact drills. Follow these basic rules to avoid injury and to encourage fair play:

* Cut finger- and toenails short to prevent scratching.
* Take off jewelry and earrings.
* Tap twice or pinch as a signal to release.
* Always practice under an instructor's supervision.
* Do not kick, bite, scratch, or punch.
* Start each drill when the instructor says "go," and end when the instructor says "break" or blows the whistle.

Shoulder Push Drill. This is a good warm-up drill for two people. Treading in deep water, face each other. Place your hands on each other's shoulders (one arm inside, one arm outside). Your hands cannot leave the shoulder area. When the instructor says "go," try to push your partner's head underwater. As soon as one person is completely submerged, the other person wins the drill. Winning is not as important as developing your water awareness with another person.

Note to instructors: This drill can be done on an individual team (two people) basis in groups. To experience with different skill levels, you may pair up the group, start the drill, then switch partners around and repeat. Keep the initial introduction to one or two rounds, but increase it as your group gets stronger. This drill should take no more than 5 min.

Circle Duck Drill. This drill is for training lifeguards to suck, tuck, and duck—a very important part of handling releases properly. Form a circle in the deep water away from the edge of the pool. Then count off. Number *1*, *2*, and *3* go to the center as "victims." Everyone else designated as "rescuers" turn around to face out. The middle three randomly try to get the people facing outward in a rear head hold. The outside rescuers try to take a quick breath, turn the head to the side, and duck under, but not release. The object is not to get caught in a grasp under the neck and to respond correctly.

Note to instructors: After numbers *1*, *2*, and *3* have been victims for 30 seconds to a minute, call *4*, *5*, and *6*; then *7*, *8*, and *9*, and so on. Give everyone an opportunity to get in the middle and be the victim. Do this drill in two to three sessions, taking no more than 5 minutes each time.

Double-Grip-on-One-Arm Drill. Partners face each other, treading in deep water. One partner (the victim) grabs the other's (rescuer) arm with both hands. The object for the victim is not to let go for any reason until absolutely necessary. The rescuer is to release the grip and place the victim in a control tow as quickly as he or she can. Wait until the instructor says "go" to start.

Note to instuctors: Allow partners 30 seconds to a minute to release the grip. Do this drill in groups of pairs. Have participants switch partners so that they can work with different people. Attempt this drill after the participants have learned the double-grip-on-one-arm release; have them do this several times so transfer of releases can take place.

Rescue/Victim Drill. Face each other, treading in deep water. Designate one partner as a victim whose purpose is to get the rescuer in any hold possible (rear head, front head, body scissors, etc.); the rescuer must defend and release the holds and get the victim in a control tow.

Shark's Circle Drill. *Note to instructors:* This drill demands a higher level of skill. Have a group of 6 to 10 people make a circle, treading in deep water. Have them count off so that each person has a number. Then call out two random numbers, for example Number 1 to the middle, and Number 2 charge Number 1. Those two people go to the middle of the circle; one attempts to put the other in a cross-chest control carry for three seconds. After approximately 15 to 20 seconds, call time and call another number to charge Number 1. After Number 1 has been in the middle for 2 or 3 rounds, the instructor calls another number to the middle for several rounds. Mix up the numbers. As the group builds endurance, members should be able to stay in the middle up to 8 rounds. This drill combines the skills in all the other drills.

One on One Drill.   Treading in deep water, start by facing each other with your hands on each other's shoulders. When the instructor says "go," let go of the shoulders and use any allowable means to secure the cross-chest control tow on your partner who tries to resist.

After saying "go," the instructor counts out loud (*1,2,3*, etc.) up to 30 seconds. If you have to stop for any reason, the instructor will stop counting and will resume counting when you begin again. You will get a 10 to 15 seconds rest during which you must put your hands back on your partner's shoulders. The drill continues until your partner has had 30 seconds to attempt the carry or has executed another pin. If done three to four times during a class, the endurance, emotional stability, and directed aggressiveness developed in this drill can help you develop confidence in your abilities.

Note to instructors: If you have a class that has participants of a variety of sizes, strengths, and abilities, you might want to modify this drill by placing two smaller guards against one larger one. This will make the larger guard work harder and come closer to simulating the effort exerted in a real situation.

Review Questions

1. List 15 of the 20 responsibilities of a lifeguard.
2. (a) List three purposes of communication, and (b) describe what makes them appropriate for the aquatic situation.
3. How does public relations relate to the responsibilities of a lifeguard?
4. Explain the basic principle behind the development of watermanship drills.

chapter 7

LIFEGUARD ADMINISTRATION

To prevent accidents you will have to become familiar with the potential dangers that are inherent in your particular area. Once you have identified danger areas, you must develop and enforce a specific rule to protect swimmers from experiencing a potential danger firsthand. These rules, however, are only guidelines and at some point you will have to determine how seriously the rule has been violated and what course of action you should take. The disciplinary actions you take will depend on the age group and on the situation regarding the rule violation. Examples of possible disciplinary actions include making the violator (a) sit out, (b) walk around the pool, (c) count tiles on the wall, (d) pick up paper, and (e) expulsion from the area.

Suggested Rules

Rules are made to protect the safety of all the swimmers in your area. Consider the following suggested rules as guidelines for designated danger areas.

Danger Areas

Certain areas are more dangerous than others as a source for potential accidents. The dangerous areas where accidents are most likely to occur are depicted in Figure 7.1. These areas must be watched closely.

Entrance. The desire to get into the water as quickly as possible leads swimmers to run from the entrance to the water. Do *not* allow running at any time in any part of the area.

Suggested rule: *NO RUNNING*

Pool deck. Running is again the prime danger on the deck area surrounding the water. Many falls resulting in injuries have occurred from running. The runner not only endangers him- or herself but the other patrons into whom he might bump or skid as well. Be firm in enforcing the *No Running* rule. Pushing and horseplay are equally dangerous.

Suggested rule: *NO RUNNING, PUSHING, OR HORSE-PLAY*

Bathers lying on deck. All swimmers sitting down or sunbathing should be at least 6 ft from the water's edge to allow for a clear passageway. Accidents happen when swimmers walking around the pool stumble or trip over those bathers lying too close to the edge on the decks.

Suggested rule: *NO SUNBATHING NEAR THE EDGE OF THE POOL*

Breakables. Bottles of suntan lotion, soft drink bottles, goggles, or masks all pose a problem in terms of possible breakage on the deck or beach or in the water. aluminum pails and tabs from

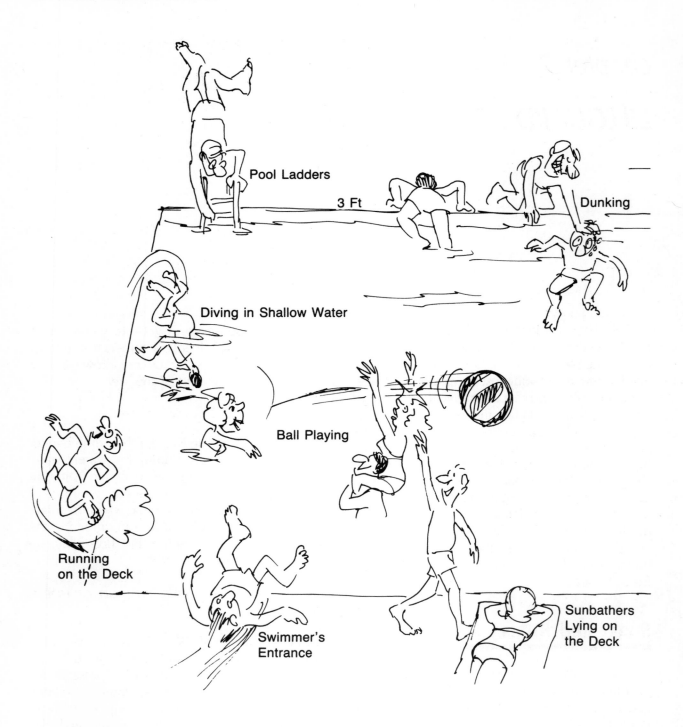

Pool Ladders

3 Ft

Dunking

Diving in Shallow Water

Ball Playing

Running on the Deck

Swimmer's Entrance

Sunbathers Lying on the Deck

7.1   Pool danger areas

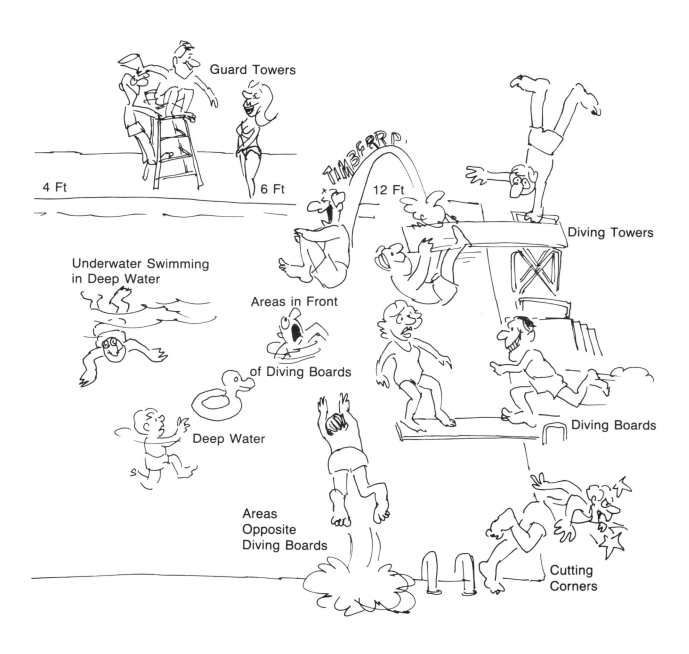

Guard Towers

4 Ft   6 Ft   12 Ft

Diving Towers

Underwater Swimming
in Deep Water

Areas in Front

of Diving Boards

Diving Boards

Deep Water

Areas
Opposite
Diving Boards

Cutting
Corners

soft drink cans have sharp edges and may also cause injury.

Suggested rule: *NO GLASS OR METAL OBJECTS IN SUPERVISED AREA*

Ladders. The ladders should not be used for diving or gymnastics. They are usually so slippery that such stunts are extremely dangerous. In addition, weak or inexperienced swimmers often use ladders to climb to the bottom. These beginners may get caught in a rung, be shoved off the ladder, or get stepped on. Such swimmers may find that they are unable to handle themselves in deep water. The ladders should be used only for climbing in and out of the water, with the user always facing the ladder.

Suggested rule: *NO PLAYING ON LADDERS*

Pool troughs. The pool overflow troughs or gutters have several dangers. The nonswimming gutter crawler depends on the pool troughs to travel from shallow to deep water; he or she will use the hand-over-hand method when the guard is looking the other way. The danger arises when the swimmer attempts to climb out of the water and traps a knee or elbow in the gutter. Bending the trapped joint will usually free it if an angle is formed that offers little or no resistance. Use of soap on the joint may also help free the individual.

Suggested rules:

- *NONSWIMMERS MUST STAY IN SHALLOW WATER*
- *USE THE LADDERS TO EXIT THE POOL*

Floatlines. The chief danger to watch for involves small children or weak swimmers who edge into deep water hand over hand along the buoy lines (or pool gutters). If accidentally pushed or otherwise separated from the lines, they are beyond their depth and consequently in danger. Additionally, swimmers should not sit or hang on floatlines as it is more difficult for the distressed swimmer to find the line to use as a temporary support.

Suggested rules:

- *NO SITTING OR HANGING ON FLOATLINES*
- *NONSWIMMERS IN SHALLOW WATER ONLY*

Diving boards and towers. Many of the accidents associated with diving can be prevented. Diving is not excessively dangerous if the lifeguard is alert to certain possibilities and acts accordingly. Some of the many causes for diving accidents include the condition and arrangement of the equipment and diving areas, the visibility into the water, and numerous weather factors. The lifeguard must check diving equipment regularly throughout the day as part of his patrol pattern. Rules for the use of diving stations should be posted and their observance rigidly enforced at all times.

Suggested rules:

- *MOUNT TO DIVING BOARDS BY LADDERS ONLY*
- *ONLY ONE DIVER ON THE BOARD AT A TIME*
- *DIVING FROM END OF BOARD ONLY: DIVE STRAIGHT OUT*
- *WAIT UNTIL PRECEDING DIVER SWIMS CLEAR*
- *NO DOUBLE BOUNCING*

The area enclosed by a radius approximately 15 ft from the end of the diving board and the diving tower should be buoyed off. Swimmers must be cautioned against swimming in this area and of remaining there after diving.

Suggested rules:

- *SWIM IMMEDIATELY TO THE SIDE AFTER DIVING*
- *NO SWIMMING IN AREA UNDER BOARDS*
- *NO HANGING ON BOARDS*

Shallow water. The primary dangers of shallow water are diving and dunking. The inexperienced diver may hit the bottom, causing injuries to fingers, hand, head, neck, or back. Be sure to mark all depths prominently to alert divers to the conditions.

Dunking is a common action of playful children. The unsuspecting swimmer might ingest water and become scared.

Suggested rules:

- *NO DIVING IN SHALLOW WATER*
- *NO DUNKING*

Deep-water area.   Two primary dangers in deep water are nonswimmers and underwater swimmers. The nonswimmers can be spotted sneaking to the deep water along the gutter, on the deck, or from the diving board. They have a very apprehensive look on their faces and usually have their arms folded or wrapped around them. Prevent them from getting into the deep end.

Underwater swimmers may be jumped on, thus receiving back injuries, or they may "black out" from hyperventilating. Masks, snorkels, and fins may lure poor swimmers into deep water by falsely increasing the swimmer's confidence in his or her ability and security.

Suggested rules:

- *NONSWIMMERS MUST STAY IN SHALLOW WATER*
- *NO UNDERWATER DISTANCE SWIMMING*
- *NO UNDERWATER SWIMMING IN DIVING AREA*
- *EQUIPMENT NOT PERMITTED FOR DEEP-WATER USE*

Water area in general.   Inner tubes, plastic toys, or similar devices can be a hazard in the water, especially in crowded areas or on windy days. The lifeguard may prohibit the use of these items within the swimming area. To improve the safety of the area, nonswimmers should be confined to shallow water. Parents who choose to augment their child's swim lessons may provide flotation devices for their child. However, infants and nonswimmers must be accompanied by an adult. Parents have an obligation to assist the work of the lifeguard.

Suggested rules:

- *NO FLOATING AIDS OR AIR MATTRESSES*
- *ADULT SUPERVISION REQUIRED FOR ALL NON-SWIMMERS AND CHILDREN UNDER 6*

Lifeguard towers and equipment. Towers present a hazard because they, by their nature,

are an allurement to young children. Ring buoys or other safety devices may prove equally attractive and dangerous. A ring buoy could prove dangerous as a floating aid to a foolhardy nonswimmer.

Suggested rules:

- *NO CLIMBING ON GUARD TOWERS*
- *EMERGENCY EQUIPMENT FOR LIFEGUARD USE ONLY*

Although the preceding suggestions may alert the lifeguard to many potential accidents, each swimming area presents unique difficulties and requires creative, concrete formulation of rules for effective prevention. To a large degree, the lifeguard must decide where the primary danger points are located: That is, what may potentially be the most dangerous point in one area is not necessarily the most dangerous in another. Study your layout and acquaint yourself with the different problems that your pool or waterfront presents; then combat these problems by developing and enforcing specific safety rules.

Special Situations

The following are some special situations often overlooked:

Intoxicated person.   It is not advisable to have intoxicated persons in or around the facility. Prohibit intoxicating beverages or intoxicated persons from entering the facility, and ask intoxicated persons to leave the area altogether. Call the police if the manager or the assistant manager cannot handle this situation. If you have assessed a person as being intoxicated, try to encourage him or her to have someone take him or her home. Do not allow this person to drive from your facility in an inebriated condition.

Disturbances.   Disturbances originating outside the jurisdiction of the guard (beyond the fence-containing area) and affecting patrons of the facility should be referred to the proper authorities.

Thievery. Conspicuously post notices regarding responsibility for personal property. However, personnel should be alert to any thievery. Do not accuse a person of theft unless you have positive proof and witnesses present. There is danger of libel if you cannot substantiate your accusation. Make sure you have filled out the appropriate incident report and obtained statements from witnesses.

Petting or necking. Do not permit this type of conduct. Diplomatically control these situations from the start of the swimming season.

Indecent Exposure. This is a crime in most areas. If someone indecently exposes him- or herself, diplomatically suggest to this person to cover up or you will call the proper authorities.

Drugs. Drugs are a rapidly growing problem. Users can be prone to accidents and drownings. Be aware of signs and behavior patterns of drug users. (Signs could include dilated pupils, rapid pulse, elevated blood pressure, nervousness, and erratic behavior, depending on the drugs abused.)

Emergency Procedures

The "accident," by definition, can never be foreseen precisely; however, being generally prepared for common types of emergencies will help reduce the stress and guesswork when an emergency does occur. Practice the sequence of steps to take during common accidents. Think through them as you practice and think of ways to adapt them in other circumstances.

Emergency Policy Guidelines

Every facility is strongly encouraged to document its emergency procedures prior to any emergency; these procedures can only enhance the quality of the aquatic program and the training of new personnel. An emergency action plan flow chart is presented in Appendix C. If you work for a facility that does not have these procedures documented, strongly encourage the man-

agement to follow these guidelines and develop a policy that includes:

- specifying who should be involved and establishing a sequence of emergency steps,
- defining the scope and content of the first-aid treatment,
- defining personnel responsible during emergency situations; give job description and define limitations,
- listing emergency phone numbers,
- defining the procedures for moving or transporting victims,
- defining the limits of liability insurance,
- instructing lifeguards in filling out incident reports and specifying to whom the reports should be returned. A sample Incident Report form is included in Appendix D.

Minor First Aid

The procedure for providing first aid for small cuts, scrapes, and burns that require prompt attention is as follows:

1. Signal (calling, hand signals) another guard to cover the area during treatment of the injury.
2. Assess the injury and administer first aid.
3. Calmly notify parents or guardians of the injured person.
4. Refer injured person to medical personnel if necessary.
5. Fill out incident report, turn it in to the appropriate person, and return to duty.

Swimmer in Difficulty

If a swimmer is in difficulty in a pool or supervised area, give an emergency signal, alerting other lifeguards who will then take over supervision of the pool area, assist in rescue or removal, send for any first-aid equipment that may be needed (blanket, resuscitator, etc.), control the onlookers, and, if necessary, clear the deck area where the rescue is being made.

If you discover that the victim's difficulties are due to some illness requiring immediate specialized attention (e.g., heart attack, seizure, or stroke), then begin major first aid immediately.

If you bring the victim to the side and determine that the accident is due to panic, overexertion, a cramp, or to swallowing water, you should

- give the appropriate first aid,
- watch for shock,
- send the victim for a medical check-over,
- make a complete report, and
- return to duty as soon as the victim has been cleared and your report has been completed.

Missing Persons

Here again it must be emphasized that these safety procedures should be practiced ahead of time. Being prepared is essential for preventing as well as reacting to an emergency. The search procedure for an average-sized pool is somewhat simpler than that for a public beach, camp waterfront, or larger pool and may be dealt with more simply. Search techniques were discussed at length in chapter 5.

With any report of a missing person (a) begin an immediate pool check, (b) signal the other guards to an emergency, and (c) get an accurate description of the possible victim, including age, height, color of hair, color of clothing, and last place he or she was seen. If necessary, evacuate the pool. Do a visual search around the edge of the pool as quickly as possible. If the missing person has become a drowning victim, make the rescue and begin major first aid immediately. If it is determined that the missing person is not a victim of drowning, then swimming may resume while the following steps are taken in order.

1. Check all facilities including washrooms, locker rooms, gymnasiums, and any other related facility.
2. Check the missing person's home by phone.
3. Notify the police. (This is the duty of the manager or head lifeguard.)

Pool Maintenance

Each individual aquatic facility will have its own system and procedure for maintaining the actual water environment of the pool. Even though these systems will vary, all should nevertheless meet the standards set by the appropriate governmental public health and safety organization. Become familiar with your facility's system.

Filtration Equipment

In general, the filtration system in pools is designed to recirculate the water constantly, keeping it clean, safe, and enjoyable for all swimmers. The functions of the system include:

- removal of coarse material such as hair, lint, and leaves, which will otherwise interfere with subsequent treatment process;
- addition of fresh water to make up for water lost by leakage, splashing, evaporation, cleaning, and skimming the pool;
- recirculation by pumping so that all pool water passes through the treatment process at least once every 6 or 8 hours;
- addition of chlorine for disinfecting the water;
- addition of alum to aid filtration;
- addition of soda ash or acid, when needed, to maintain the pH level;
- filtration to remove any suspended matter in the water; and
- provisions for reversing the flow of water through the filters to remove the filtered material and dispose of it in the sewer.

The system consists of a hair and lint catcher that functions to remove hair, lint, and other foreign matter from the water. It has a decided economic value in that it protects the pumping unit. If this foreign material is allowed to pass through the recirculating system, it not only causes excessive wear on the pump, but becomes embedded in the filter sand to such an extent that backwashing may not remove it.

Pumps and motors complete the filtration system. Repairs on the pumps and motors should always be made by competent repairmen who are familiar with the instructions of the manufacturer regarding their equipment. Normal maintenance will consist of (a) protecting the pumps and motors against corrosion of metal or electrical parts caused by contact with the water and chemicals, (b) lubricating according to the manufacturer's specifications, and (c) adjusting the pump packing to ensure that there is a slight leak, thus avoiding overtightening the adjustment bolts.

Disinfecting Pool Water

Several procedures are available to disinfect pool water. Some processes are more prominent than others. Ultraviolet rays, for example, were used extensively in the early development of swimming pools for disinfecting but are now obsolete. Although they have great disinfecting qualities, ultraviolet rays are good only at the point of contact and cannot be retained in the water to take care of the organisms in the pool properly.

Chlorine is the most widely used disinfectant. Chlorine acts quickly, and a residual can be maintained in the water for continuous disinfection. The corrosive and poisonous nature of the element does create difficulty in distribution and handling.

Chlorination can be accomplished in several ways. Pure chlorine contained in cylinders under pressure is used as gas. It is the cheapest method of providing chlorine, except that an expensive chlorinator must be installed to feed the gas. Hypochlorites in liquid or powder form can also be used, added by chemical feeder. However, continuous application of chlorine is necessary in order to maintain a steady residual.

The water must also be tested for chlorine residual. Water is considered safe if a minimal residual of .4 ppm (parts per million) can be maintained. Most authorities recommend a residual of .4 ppm to .6 ppm. These values are general and may vary from state to state. Check with your local health department for your specific health standards.

Another method used to test residual is the colorimeter test method. Test kits are available from many sources. A sample of water to be tested is mixed with the test solution in a test tube. The immediate coloring produced indicates the amount of residual chlorine present. By comparing the color on a fixed scale, an accurate reading can be made in a matter of seconds. These testing kits are known as colorimeters.

Filtration

Dirt and particulate material must be removed from swimming pool water to provide for maximum water clarity. Two basic types of filtration, sand and gravel filters and diatomaceous earth filters, are used to remove particulate matter.

Sand and gravel filters.   Three types of sand and gravel filters are utilized in YMCA swimming pools. They are vacuum, pressure sand, and high pressure sand filters.

- *Vacuum*. This filter consists of a bed of several layers of sand and gravel. The tank is open at the top and water is drawn (vacuumed) by a pump through the layers of sand and gravel (top to bottom) and returned to the pool.
- *Pressure sand*. Several layers of sand and gravel are contained in a closed filter tank. Water is forced (pushed) through the media, with particulate matter being trapped on the surface of the top layer of sand.
- *High pressure sand*. Two or more small, closed filter tanks, usually consisting of a few feet of sand on top of a layer of gravel, are used to produce a faster flow rate. Dirt particles are removed throughout the entire bed of sand (deep penetration) as water moves through the filter from top to bottom.

Vacuum and pressure sand filter capabilities are usually enhanced by adding aluminum sulfate to the filter tank. The alum "flocs" the filter (forms a gelatin-like material) on the top layer of sand. An alum floc enables the filter to remove body oils and minute dirt particles.

When sand filters become dirty, the pump and motor are required to work harder to move water through the filter. If the filter is not cleaned when necessary the motor may burn out, causing expensive maintenance or replacement. Sand filters are backwashed (cleaned) by manipulating the valves within the circulation system in accordance with the manufacturer's specifications. Water is withdrawn from the pool and forced slowly through the filter in the opposite direction from which it normally flows (bottom to top). Filter tanks are cleaned one at a time. After cleaning alum is replaced in the filter and make up water is added to the pool.

Diatomaceous earth filters. Diatomaceous earth is a filter medium comprised of fossilized marine plant life (diatoms). When diatomaceous earth is applied to the system's filter elements, water passes through and around the tiny spaces in the diatoms, trapping the dirt particles on the surface. Diatomaceous earth filters, because of the size of their individual particles, are capable of removing matter much smaller than sand filters. Two types of diatomaceous earth filters are used in YMCA pools, vacuum and pressure.

- *Vacuum diatomaceous earth.* As with vacuum sand filters, water is drawn (vacuumed) through the filter elements covered with the diatomaceous earth. These elements are contained in an open tank. Dirt (particle matter) is trapped on the diatomaceous earth along the entire surface of the elements. A pressure switch automatically turns off the motor when pressure builds to a predetermined level.

- *Pressure diatomaceous earth.* Filter elements are contained in a closed tank. A viewing port is usually built into the side of the tank that allows observation of a few elements to determine how well they are coated. Water is forced (pushed) through all sides of the element, trapping dirt on the surface of the diatomaceous earth. When the pressure of the water entering the filter tank reaches the maximum level specified by the manufacturer, the filter must be cleaned.

A diatomaceous earth filter cycle may be extended by dropping the media off of the elements and reapplying it, as diatomaceous earth is reusable. Eventually it must be removed from the filter and new media must be added. In a vacuum system the old coat is purged from the elements by rinsing them off with a hose after the water has been removed from the filter tank. With a pressure system the flow of water is reversed through the elements and the old diatomaceous

earth is completely purged from the filter tank with water from the pool.

The Acidity—Base Balance (pH)

The proper acidity-base balance is important in pool operation for three reasons:

1. For effective coagulation of alum
2. For effective use of chlorine as a disinfectant
3. For minimum irritation to swimmers' eyes and skin

This balance is maintained by testing for pH. When alum is used, sulfuric acid is formed as a by-product and has a tendency to produce an acid reaction to the water. When this happens, proper floccing of alum is not possible. The alum goes into solution and enters the pool, causing irritation to swimmers and turbidity to the water. The pH test is used to monitor the water for such difficulties by using a colorimeter. A rating below 7.0 is considered acidic; above 7.0, base. The water must be maintained alkaline at all times for the proper operation of the filtering plant. It is recommended that the pH be maintained at 7.4 to 7.6 for optimum operation. Soda ash (sodium carbonate) is the generally accepted material used to raise the alkalinity whenever it is necessary. It can be fed into the pool water by a chemical feeder.

Algae Control

Control of algae has been one of the most perplexing problems to the swimming pool operator. Although it is seldom a problem in indoor installations, outdoor pools are confronted with algae (plant life introduced into the water by wind and rain) all the time. If the conditions are ripe, within 24 to 48 hours algae growth can multiply sufficiently to make the water appear green or brown and cause a slimy growth on the interior of the pool structure. If an algae problem takes root, it can cause an imbalance in pool operation. The chief method for the control of algae is superchlorination of the water raising the chlorine residual to over 2.0 ppm. This must be done at night or when the pool is not in use.

Cleaning the Floor of the Pool

The filters remove the fine dirt that is held in suspension in the water; however, a certain amount of the foreign material in the water will settle to the bottom of the pool and will not be carried out in the normal recirculation process. This sediment is picked up by use of a vacuum that can be used without emptying the pool. Thus great expense and time of operation is saved. Two general types of cleaners include a portable pump and motor, which can be rolled to the edge of the pool, and a vacuum line hooked up to the recirculation system. The vacuum line hook-up can be operated without any loss of water. Connections to the vacuum hose are made by outlets at various points around the pool that are situated a few inches under the surface of the water.

Other models and methods are on the market, and information about them is available at your local pool store. The best time to vacuum is in the morning when no one is in the pool and when sediment has had a chance to settle. In smaller pools the operation can be done from the deck by the use of long handles. In larger pools, the cleaner can be dragged across the floor by means of a rope. A well-vacuumed pool will aid greatly in maintaining an attractive pool and will also take a load off the filters.

Temperature Control

For typical conditions, the pool water should not be warmer than 82° F. The minimum temperature should be 78° F. Certain aquatic programs require water temperatures up to 86° F, such as those for people with arthritis, multiple sclerosis, or handicaps, or for senior citizens. Warm water encourages growth of both bacteria and algae. Where the air temperature can be controlled, it should be at least the equal of water temperature and preferably a few degrees higher for comfort.

Record Keeping

Maintaining proper records is a must in order to keep your facility running smoothly on a daily basis. Many state and municipal public health departments require that records be kept for many reasons. As long as the reports are maintained and organized properly, you can refer back to them if there is a question on procedure. Proper records also make training new personnel easier, and in case of a lawsuit, your records are probably the best defense of your actions.

Checklists

Forms like the one shown in Appendix E should be designed to include all the areas that lifeguards should check on a regular basis. These areas may vary depending on the type of facility you are guarding; however, the forms should include the name of the facility, date, areas to be checked, time of day the areas are checked, and the signature of the person who checked them. As a guideline, the areas below should be listed on the form. You may need to add or subtract to the list, depending on your facility.

- bottom
- clarity of water
- chemical reading
- air and water temperature
- deck
- ladders
- lane ropes
- first-aid kit
- safety equipment
- lights
- circulation system
- diving board area
- exit doors
- water fountains
- deck chairs/furniture
- drains

Pool Danger Zones

As shown in Figure 7.1 on pages 90-91, each pool has certain areas that are more prone to accidents than others. The following areas are considered the danger zones and should be watched more closely:

- in front of diving board
- at the drop off point

- ladders
- under the diving board
- the diving board
- deck
- play area
- shallow end
- deep end
- lockers
- entrance and exit doors
- water fountains
- trough
- under lifeguard chair

Be sure to watch these areas *carefully* as you scan your assigned areas.

Incident Reports

As a professional, you are responsible for your decisions. Maintaining good written records of daily routines in addition to incident reports are the only ways available in many instances to substantiate your procedures and action if they are ever questioned.

In case of any accident that requires you to clear the pool, effect a rescue, or secure transportation to an emergency facility, your responsibility does not end with the injured person being delivered to the appropriate party for additional medical care. Make sure that you follow your facility's procedures for reporting and recording the incident. Those procedures should include filing the following information and answers to the questions in a format that best services your facility:

- Names, titles, employment numbers, number of seasons employed as lifeguard, location of assignment, tour of duty and lunch period of employees involved. Date, type, and amount of training in lifeguard techniques.
- Time, location, and nature of the accident.
- Number of persons involved in accident.
- Condition of water and weather.
- Population of beach or pool where accident took place.
- How did the employee become aware of accident?
- How soon did the employee respond to the emergency situation?

- What did the employee do in response to the emergency situation?
  1. Did the guard have to enter the water to effect a rescue?
  2. How far did the guard have to swim?
  3. Did the guard get any assistance?
  4. Did anything interfere with the rescue?
  5. Did the guard do everything possible to help revive the victim?
- Was the victim identified? By whom?
- What were the contributing factors?
  1. What was the victim doing at time of distress?
  2. Could the victim swim?
  3. Had the victim disregarded rules or orders given by the lifeguard?
- Was cardiopulmonary resuscitation necessary?
  1. Was effective circulation noted in carotid pulse, pupil reflex, and skin color?
  2. If a resuscitator was employed in conjunction with CPR, did the equipment have a manual override?
- Was resuscitator used?
  1. Was it available on location or did it have to be brought to the scene?
  2. What means of artificial respiration was used prior to use of the resuscitator?
- Were police, emergency squad, and ambulance called?
  1. How soon did they respond?
  2. What action did they take?
  3. Was artificial respiration continued? By whom?
  4. When did the paramedic or doctor take over?
  5. When did the paramedic or doctor make declaration as to the victim's condition?
  6. Was the victim removed from the beach or pool area? What time?
- General comment of employees involving anything about the case that might have been overlooked.
- Plan or sketch of area showing any unusual conditions, and assignments of personnel if, in the opinion of the interviewer, it is necessary. This sketch should be prepared by supervisor.

A sample Incident Form is included in the Appendix on page 109. This form is meant as a guideline and should be amended to meet the needs of your facility.

Pool Management and the Law: General Legal Information

Most cases involving swimming pools involve the law of torts. Liability arises when one fails to perform an action that should have been performed or when someone performs an incorrect action, either one of which results in injury. Cases involving swimming pools generally focus on one of the following two legal elements that give rise to liability: negligence and nuisance. Specific laws regarding aquatic liability will vary from state to state. Check with the appropriate departments in your local government to find out the specific laws governing swimming pool safety in your area.

Negligence

Negligence can be defined as "actions that fall below the standard established by law for the protection of others against unreasonable risks of harm." The following elements are necessary for a course of action based on negligence:

1. A legal duty to conform to a standard of conduct for the protection of others against unreasonable risks.
2. A failure to conform to this standard (breach of duty) after being placed on notice or reason to foresee the accident.
3. A reasonably close causal connection (legally called *Proximate Cause*) between the conduct and the resulting injury.

4. An actual loss or damage resulting to the interests of another. Damage must be shown: If a person is as good after the injury as before the injury, he or she would sustain no injury and hence negligence would not be charged.

What is the degree of care provided by a lifeguard? or What is the lifeguard's duty? Lifeguards don't insure the safety of patrons. If, in the exercise of his or her duty, an accident occurs, he or she must function in a competent manner; that is, the lifeguard must function within the standards established by the organization that certified him or her. If he or she acts according to those standards, there will be no liability. If he or she does *not* and something is omitted or done improperly, he or she can be held liable.

What is the degree of care provided by a manager? The manager must see to it that games, slides, diving boards, and such are safe. He or she should be sure that the diving area is properly marked and that the water is deep enough for novice diving. If you are the supervisor, indicate what should and should not be done. For example, if it is not your job to test the water, then don't do it. Make sure, however, that it is tested by someone before you go on duty.

Giving constructive notice. What is your knowledge, or constructive notice, in being liable? In the area that you control, it is your job to know of any dangerous conditions that may exist, regardless of whether or not you have actual knowledge of them. If an employee sees a hazardous condition but fails to report it to the employer, the employer is considered to have constructive notice because he or she should have been aware of the condition. Hence, the employer can be held liable.

In any situation, a duty is imposed upon the owner of the facility, whether public or private, to keep the premises safe. The owner must ensure the following items:

- Chemicals and storage areas are safely and properly used.
- Rescue equipment is in good working order and in plain sight.
- Ladders and diving structures are safe and in good repair.
- Lighting, including underwater lights, is safe and adequate.
- Pool water is sanitized: chlorine and pH levels correctly adjusted.
- Water is clear.
- Pool depth is clearly marked at all places where the depth might change, especially the shallow and deep ends.
- Regular checks are made for hazards such as broken glass, equipment that has not been put away, or cracked cement around back posts of the diving structure.

Degree or standard of care. A lifeguard is obligated to use the care that the circumstances would indicate to ordinary prudent and careful persons. Legal liability for negligence is based upon conduct involving unreasonable risk to another. This risk must be established by showing that such conduct falls below the standard represented by the conduct of reasonable persons under the same or similar circumstances. In determining whether care has been exercised under similar circumstances, inquiry should be made into matters within the realm of general information. The action or inaction that will amount to ordinary care depends on the facts or circumstances of each particular case.

Nuisance

Nuisance is not the same as negligence. Nuisance is defined as anything that causes hurt, inconvenience, annoyance, or damage. As an example, courts have held that the mere operation of a swimming pool is not a nuisance if it is operated without disturbing its surroundings. However, if large floodlights are used or noisy parties are held and they disturb others, this may be considered a nuisance.

In essence, you must exercise the duties of reasonable care. While there are numerous ways you can be held liable for an injury, the only sure way to avoid liability is to see that the accident doesn't occur. By taking the appropriate actions to ensure the safety of the patrons of your facility, adhering to the state regulations regarding pool standards and safety, and obtaining the appropriate liability insurance to protect yourself and your facility against liability, you have done as much prior preparation as is possible to prevent accidents from occurring.

Review Questions

1. Why should swimmers not be allowed to dive into shallow water?
2. List the procedure for (a) a minor accident resulting in a cut or scrape, (b) a swimmer in distress, or (c) a missing person.
3. What is the function of a pool maintenance system?
4. Explain the basic flow of a pool's filter system.
5. Why is the acidity/alkalinity balance important to the operation of the pool system?
6. Define negligence in regard to pool management.
7. Define nuisance in regard to pool management.
8. List two ways to avoid being found liable.

appendix A

AQUATIC SAFETY

The Aquatic Safety course is an introduction to water safety and is structured to reach a wide audience with no previous training in aquatic safety. This course has no specific prerequisites and is designed to adapt to the needs of individuals in different aquatic settings. The course can be adapted to be incorporated into a corporate fitness program setting as well as geared to backyard pool safety or to families who attend aquatic areas for recreation or vacation. Nonswimmers are encouraged to enroll and participate (to the extent that they are able) to increase their aquatic safety knowledge.

The course consists of 8 hours of classroom and possible water sessions, depending on the scope of the class offered.

The course outline includes discussions of the following:

1. History and philosophy of YMCA aquatic safety and lifeguarding training
2. Personal aquatic safety information
3. General aquatic information
4. Accident prevention principles
5. Basic survival skills and principles
6. Basic first aid and rescusitation demonstration
7. Nonswimming rescues

Testing and certification are administered on a local basis using a written or oral test. A water test requiring successful completion of a 100-yard swim in any style, a 3-minute survival float in a front or back float position, a jump into the water and recovery of an object from the bottom of a 6 to 8 ft depth, and a demonstration of the proper use of three basic rescue techniques are also required. Certification for aquatic safety and additional certificates of participation are issued by local YMCAs.

appendix B

YMCA LIFEGUARD TRAINING PROGRAM

The YMCA lifeguard training program is designed to train skilled lifeguards and prepare them for the professionally demanding occupation of a lifeguard. The course emphasizes the preventative concepts of guarding, lifesaving skills for contact rescues, communication, public relations, and administrative skills, in addition to refined watermanship skills. It provides the professional lifeguard with a basic awareness of different types of aquatic environments and a general knowledge of aquatic science. This course is a prerequisite course for YMCA Aquatic Leadership Training Programs.

To participate in the program, the following prerequisites must be met:

- Participants must be at least 16 years old.
- Participants must pass the following swimming test.
  1. An endurance swim on a 20 to 25-yd course, consisting of ¼ mi of the lifesaving medley, and at least two lengths of each of the following:
     - sidestroke on both sides
     - approach crawl
     - elementary backstroke
     - lifesaving stroke on both sides
     - breaststroke approach
     - legs alone for elementary backstroke, breaststroke, and scissors kick
  2. Survival float for a total of 20 min—10 min each of hands only and feet only.
  3. Tread water for at least 2 min with arms only and 2 min with legs only.
  4. Surface dive, head first and feet first, in 8 to 10 ft of water.
  5. Swim underwater for 20 yd.
- Participants must have a CPR certification prior to completing the lifeguarding course.

The course includes 28 to 36 hours of classroom and pool practice sessions. The course outline includes the following topics:

1. Introduction and importance of aquatic safety
2. Personal safety including basic survival skills, swimming strokes, and nonswimming strokes
3. Aquatic information about environments and science
4. Aquatic rescues including situation assessment, use of rescue equipment, and swimming rescues
5. Special situations that include handling of spinal injuries, rescue breathing, scuba rescue, ice rescue, submerged vehicle escape, search patterns, and basic first aid
6. Lifeguard responsibilities and administration that includes duties, conditioning, suggested rules and emergency procedures, reports, and pool maintenance.

Testing and certification will be based on completion of the 28- to 36-hour course and passing a written or oral knowledge test, plus a practical skills test. Certification is reported to the Aquatics Division of the National YMCA (YMCA of the USA, 101 North Wacker Drive, Chicago, IL 60606). The certification is renewable every 2 years through your local YMCA. Lifeguard certification is conducted by a *certified lifeguard instructor*. If you are interested in becoming a lifeguard instructor, consult the Field Aquatic Coordinator for training information.

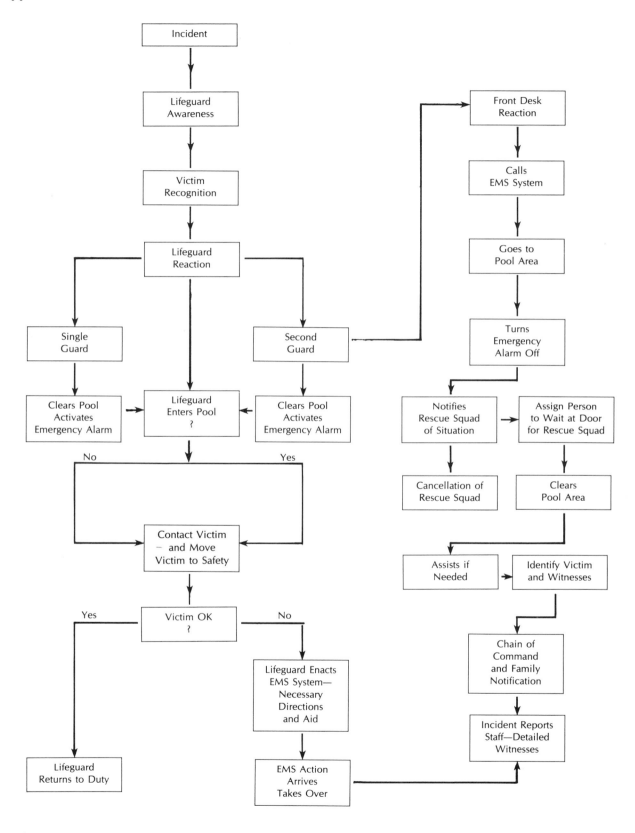

*Prepared by the Klamath County YMCA Pool Administrators.

Date of report _____

Name of injured person _____ Age _____

Address _____ Phone _____

Occupation _____ Employed by _____

Date of accident _____ Time _____

Location _____

What was injured person doing when hurt? _____

Number of persons involved _____ Names _____

_____

Water condition _____ Weather condition _____

Population of pool or beach _____

Swimming ability of victim _____

Did victim disregard rules or order of lifeguard? _____ Explain _____

_____

Was a resuscitator used? _____ How long? _____

Means of artificial respiration prior to resuscitator? _____ How long? _____

Was cardiopulmonary resuscitation used? _____ How long? _____

Where was injured taken after accident? _____ Doctor _____

Were police or ambulance emergency squad called? _____

Time of arrival _____ Action taken _____

Name of lifeguard assisting in rescue _____ Position _____

Number of seasons employed as lifeguard _____ Location of assignment _____

_____

List names, addresses, and phone numbers of at least two (2) witnesses on back of this report form.

General comment of employees involved:

Sketch area of accident showing unusual conditions and assignments of personnel on back of this report form if in the opinion of the interviewer it is necessary.

Name of YMCA _____

Location of YMCA _____

Name _____

Date _____ Time _____

Section	Yes	No	Comments
Access to Pool			
Doors and gates locked when not guarded			
Entry to pool from locker rooms at the shallow end of pool			
Indoor Pools			
Separate from showers			
Showers should be passed through to get to the pool			
Doors and windows locked			
Lights checked			
Outdoor Pools			
Gates in good condition and locked			
Fences in good condition and high enough to prevent easy access			
Lights checked			
Pool Area			
Access ways to pool clear and free of obstructions			
All walking surfaces in good condition			
Rules clearly visible from all locations in pool area			
Guards enforce rules			

Section	Yes	No	Comments
Deck area free from nonskid material and free from obstructions			
Pool depth markings clearly visible on deck and in accordance with local codes			
Adequate lighting provided so all pool areas are visible			
Rescue equipment visible and available			
Equipment checked to ensure good operating condition			
Pool personnel properly trained in the handling of rescue equipment and procedure			
Keys to pool area kept in safe place			
Lifeguard Responsibilities			
Positioned so all areas of pool and its bottom are clearly visible at all times			
Control entry to pool			
Enforce all rules			
Check the availability and condition of all rescue equipment			
Emergency Procedures			
A posted emergency procedure in effect			
Emergency procedure practiced regularly			
Pool alarm system tested regularly			
Pool			
Deep water lifelines in place			
Local health codes for water posted			
All metal shall be grounded and all electrical devices connected to ground fault interrupters			
Pool temperature checked and recorded 3 times per day			

Section	Yes	No	Comments
Air temperature checked and recorded 3 times per day			
Chlorine content checked and recorded 3 times per day			
Ph of water checked and recorded 3 times per day			
Chemicals (other than chlorine) checked			
Backwash schedule checked			
Other pertinent factors checked			
Attendance checked each hour			
Diving Area			
Diving areas separated from swimming areas			
Diving rules clearly posted			
Handrails or gutters must be present and easy to reach			
Pool free of all foreign objects that cause injury			
Maintenance			
All applicable safety codes met			
Two persons present when pool is being maintained			
When pool is drained, signs posted indicating such			
Drained pool is secured in the same manner as a filled pool			
Water tests for bacteria regularly taken and documented			
Chemicals are not added directly to the pool when swimmers are present			
Chemicals stored in safe, protected area			
Chemicals handled in accordance with manufacturer's instructions and protective clothing worn when necessary			

REFERENCES

Canadian Red Cross Society. (1983). *Cold water survival*. Victoria, British Columbia: Author.

Kuhn, B. (1961). In American Red Cross-Klamath Basin Chapter (Ed.), *Submerged vehicle study*. Unpublished manuscript.

Nemiroff, M.J. (1979, October). Cold water near-drowning. *Journal of Physical Education and Recreation*, 76-77.

Nemiroff, M.J. (1982, November). *Survival following cold water near-drowning*. Paper presented at the conference for the Council for National Cooperation in Aquatics (CNCA), Columbus, OH.

Silvia, C.E. (1965). *Lifesaving and water safety today*. New York: Association Press.

United States Coast Guard, Department of Transportation. (1977). *Hypothermia and cold water survival—Instructor's guide*. Washington, DC: Government Printing Office.

United States Coast Guard, Department of Transportation. (1982). *Hypothermia and cold water survival*. Washington, DC: Government Printing Office.

ADDITIONAL RESOURCES

American Red Cross. (1982). *Advanced first aid and emergency care*. Garden City, NJ: Doubleday.

Arnold, C. (1979). *YMCA aquatic safety and lifesaving program*. Chicago: National YMCA Program Resources.

Byerly, S. (1978). *Victim detection*. Huntington Beach, CA: National Surf Lifesaving Association.

Cornforth, J. (1974). *National lifeguard manual*. Champaign, IL: Human Kinetics.

Ellis, J. (1985). Drowning: Mechanism and causes. *National Aquatics Journal*, **1**(3), 10-13.

Golden, F. (1985, Spring). Hypothermia and survival. *National Aquatics Journal*, **1**, 2-10.

Howes, G. (Ed.). (1968). *Lifeguard training: Principles and administration*. New York: Association Press.

Katz, J. (1981). *Swimming for total fitness*. Garden City, NJ: Doubleday.

Maloney, J.I.T. (1974). *Aquatic safety and lifesaving program*. New York: Association Press.

McDonnell, S.N., & Tarr, J.L. (1984). *Fieldbook*. Irving, TX: Boy Scouts of America.

Mebane, G.Y., & Dick, A.P. (1985). *Dan underwater diving accident manual*. Durham, NC: Duke University Press.

National Safety Council. (1981). *Safety education bulletin* (Report No. 27). chicago: Author.

National Safety Council. (1985). *Accident facts 1985 edition*. Chicago: Author.

Pia, F. (1972). *Observations on the drowning of non-swimmers*. Vancouver, British Columbia: Royal Lifesaving Society of Canada.

Royal Lifesaving Society of Canada. *Aquatic emergency care, specific rescue*, **4**, 20-23.

Smith, D.S. (1984). Notes on drowning: The misunderstood, preventable tragedy. *The Physician and Sportsmedicine*, **12**, 66-73.

Wagner, A. (1985, April). Emergency procedures for aquatic facilities. *Parks and Recreation*, 56-69.

Yorkshire, B. (1982, November). *Wave pools and lifeguarding*. Paper presented at the conference of the Council for National Cooperation in Aquatiics, Columbus, OH.